PHILIPPE MEYRIER

Horse Owners' Essential Tips

GROOMING • CARE • TACK • FACILITIES • RIDING • PASTURE

FIREFLY BOOKS

A FIREFLY BOOK

Published by Firefly Books Ltd. 2016

First printing

Publisher Cataloging-in-Publication Data (U.S.)
Names: Meyrier, Philippe, author. | Cloutier, Lise, translator.
Title: Horse owners' essential tips : care, grooming, equipment, facilities, riding, pasture (more than 500 practical ideas) / author, Philippe Meyrier ; translator, Lise Cloutier.
Description: Richmond Hill, Ontario, Canada : Firefly Books, 2016. | Originally published by Glenat Publishing, Grenoble France, 2014 as Mes Meilleures Astuces de Cavaliers Futés | Includes index. | Summary: Ideal for new and veteran horse owners, this guidebook is filled with useful tips and advice on how to care for one's horse. Tips include how to keep one's horse healthy, safe, and of course, beautiful" – Provided by publisher.
Identifiers: ISBN 978-1-77085-846-6 (paperback)
Subjects: LCSH: Horses.
Classification: LCC SF285.3M497 |DDC 636.1 – dc23

Library and Archives Canada Cataloguing in Publication
A CIP record for this title is available from Library and Archives Canada

Published in the United States by
Firefly Books (U.S.) Inc.
P.O. Box 1338, Ellicott Station
Buffalo, New York 14205

Published in Canada by
Firefly Books Ltd.
50 Staples Avenue, Unit 1
Richmond Hill, Ontario L4B 0A7

Translation: Lise Cloutier

Printed in China

Contents

Introduction

A horseshoe first and foremost belongs on a horse's hoof, and it is traditionally considered a good luck charm. But did you know that it could also be used as a trivet in your kitchen, as a door knob on an antique dresser, to frame a picture of your beloved horse or as a bracket on a sliding gate in the pasture? There are a million and one ways to use a horseshoe! It's a must-have for any handy horseback rider who wants to save money by recycling. With a few tips and tricks, it can be put to good use in the stable or in the home, much like dozens of other repurposed items.

This book contains tips and tricks that have been shared in stables through word of mouth. Read through these pages to discover (at last!) what to do with old socks, plastic bottles, pieces of string, and even used nursing bottles. Amateur do-it-yourselfers can rest assured: most of these projects are easy to do, especially thanks to the detailed drawings by horse enthusiast Philippe Meyrier. Illustrating these tips has been a delight for him, and he approached this task seriously but with a sense of humor. As he put it, "Going from horses to plastic bottles was very entertaining!" Furthermore, he believes the word DISCARD should be banned. Whether it's to save the environment or to save money, there's nothing like the three Rs!

Grooming, Care, Tack, Facilities, Riding, Pasture, Equine Crafts … Every chapter offers tips for your horse's well-being and tricks for grooming and care, for improving quality of life and optimizing the living environment, and for lowcost repairs around the stable or in the pasture to prevent injuries. You'll also find hints for yourself so you can improve your own comfort without spending a fortune!

This book is the product of years of dialog between riders, passed down from generation to generation the old-fashioned way. Now it's your turn to share your tips or bring a new twist to those you already know. When we're all driven by the same passion, we're keen to share it with others. Thanks to this book, the conversation will continue in your stables!

Pascale Desrousseaux
Picture editor: *Cheval Magazine* and *Cheval Star*,
photographer and enthusiast of all things homemade

ESSENTIAL TIPS

GROOMING

🐴 In the Buff!

With the return of spring, horses that haven't been clipped may have a hard time shedding their winter coat. It takes more than a dandy brush to make my four-legged companion look like a horse again! A groom once gave me this useful tip: use the blade of a hacksaw (not a wood-cutting saw!) as a sweat scraper and scrape in the same direction as the horse's hair. After two or three sessions, my horse's coat became shiny and smooth again. Success guaranteed!

When I first bought my pony, his coat was very dull. In spite of a balanced diet and much grooming, I just couldn't get his coat to shine. So my veterinarian suggested this simple, lowcost solution: add half a glass of sunflower oil to each ration of feed. Sunflower oil is rich in vitamin E and gives a nice shine to my pony's coat. Supplement your horse's diet for life or as needed in one-month treatments.

JUST THE RIGHT HEIGHT

When the weather gets colder, riders bundle up with a jacket and cover their horses with exercise rugs. But after a few minutes warming up in the ring, everyone starts to get hot and perspire. When it comes time to "drop the jacket," it's not a good idea to leave your things lying on the ground . . . and there's not always someone around to pick them up and put them away. In our arena, we installed a coat hook on the wall high enough to hang our jacket and exercise rug. It's a convenient way to keep our things tidy without leaving them on the ground or dismounting.

HANG IT UP!

Furniture stores and do-it-yourself centers sell inexpensive S-shaped hooks that are great for maximizing space in the stable or horse trailer. It's a great place to hang up your bridle.

TIP FOR MOMS

I use my horse's thick exercise rug in the winter and a fly sheet in the summer to cover up my child in his car seat. I wrap my child's legs with the part of the blanket that goes over the horse's back and fasten the Velcro ties behind the back of the car seat, near the top. Not only is it easy to put on and take off, but this improvised blanket won't slip when the child moves (and Mom can keep her eyes on the road!).

 # Makeshift Velcro Cleaner

It's not always easy to properly clean the Velcro closures on shin boots, bell boots or leg wraps. Regular washing will remove soil and dust from your horse's protective gear, but hair that remains stuck in the hooks and loops cause the Velcro strips to lose their grip.
Here is a foolproof way to remove them: I simply use a wire brush for dogs or cats. The brush's curved metal tips, which are normally used to untangle your pet's fur, also help remove horse hair when used to carefully scrape the Velcro closures on horse tack (which helps make them last longer).

BABY-SOFT SKIN

I was reluctant to use sponges, which are a breeding ground for germs, to clean my horse's genitals. I have since found a great trick: baby wipes. They're easy to use and smell good too!

Spotless White Stockings

I don't like to see traces of manure or mud on my horse's leg markings, so I regularly wash them with a gentle baby soap. After wetting my horse's legs (or his entire body if it's warm enough), I shampoo and rinse his limbs and pastern joint, and rub dry with a terry towel. If that's not enough, I sprinkle some chalk on the white stockings to make them really white. There you have it, a quick way to get clean white stockings!

Nice and Dry!

In the fall and winter, horses often get their lower limbs wet after working in a soggy outdoor ring or going outside after it rains. This condition can lead to cracks that are not always easy to treat when the weather turns cold. That's why it's so important to wipe down your horse's pasterns.

An old washcloth is easier to handle than a bulky towel. You can reach every inch of your horse's legs and ensure the pastern joint is perfectly dry.

ACCESS TO WATER IN WINTER

As winter approaches, my horse's drinking supply needs to be checked daily to ensure it doesn't freeze, whether it's in the water bucket in the stall or the drinking trough in the pasture. This is not always easy to do, since ice can form at any time of day. To be sure that my horse always has access to fresh water, I put a handful of straw and a large piece of wood in his water bowls. This way, the water won't entirely freeze on the surface and my companion can drink whenever he wants.

Keep Tabs on Your Hoof Pick

My horse lives in the pasture beside my house and I take care of him directly in his shelter.

I often mislay my hoof pick in the straw or long grass. If I forget it there, I'm always afraid that my horse will hurt himself if he walks or rolls on it.

Instead, I found a way to attach it to my dandy brush. I cut a piece of leather a bit wider than the handle of the hoof pick and nailed it to the back of the brush to make a little pocket. I got into the habit of tucking my hoof pick away as soon as I finished grooming my horse. A word to the wise: you need to make the pocket very tight because the leather will loosen as it gets used.

I have a very simple trick to avoid losing or forgetting my hoof pick. I attach the hoof pick to a length of baler twine threaded through two holes bored in a tennis ball. I locate the hoof pick right away because the tennis ball is so visible. You can print your name or the name of your horse on the tennis ball to give it a personal touch, or dye it a different color!

FLYAWAY HORSE HAIR

My mare's mane is quite unmanageable and falls willy-nilly on either side of her neck, which isn't very pretty! To make matters worse, she has fairly thick hair and it's a real chore to make her look beautiful.

After untangling and combing her mane, I give it a generous coat of strong-hold hair gel for humans and smooth all the hair to the same side. With this treatment, her mane becomes nice and shiny and stays in place for days. Plus she gives off a pleasant fruity smell whenever she moves. The result is great!

An Improvised Knife

When I clean out my horses' stalls, I often forget to bring a knife with me to cut the twine on the bales of hay or straw. It's not easy to open a bale without a knife when it's tied so tightly … So instead of a knife, I use another length of twine to break the twine holding the bale. I thread it under the twine on the bale and rub quickly back and forth while holding it taut. It produces enough heat to cut the twine around the bale!

IMPECCABLE HAIR AND COAT

I have a very simple trick to keep my horses' coat and hair in peak condition. I steer clear of plastic brushes, which require long strokes and break the horse's hair. Instead, I gently brush my horse's mane and tail with a boar-bristle hairbrush. To make the hairs on his tail grow faster, I cut a quarter of an inch (0.5 cm) off my horse's tail each month during the full moon. To slow down the regrowth, I clip my horses when the moon is waning. In winter, I always cover them with a blanket. Lastly, I always add two or three spoonfuls of vegetable oil to my horses' ration during the winter. This ensures that their coat stays shiny even when it's cold outside.

Soothing Sweet Almond Oil

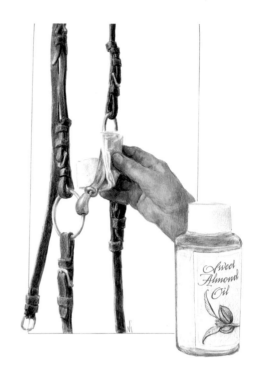

In harsh winter conditions, the corners of my horse's lips get dry, which can cause problems where the bit rubs against them. To alleviate this, I coat his mouthpiece with sweet almond oil. Its emollient and soothing properties protect the delicate skin around my horse's mouth.

Extra hint: During competitions, I apply oil all over my horse's nose. Not only does it smell good, but also makes his nose shine!

REMOVING UNWANTED HORSE HAIR

My horse perspires fairly easily and when I unsaddle him after being worked, I find the saddle pad covered in hairs. These hairs are very hard to get rid of with just a brush. Since I don't want to wash the saddle pad every day, I found a quick and easy way to remove these unwanted hairs: I spread the saddle pad on a table and shave it with a disposable razor. I scrape all the hairs off and am careful to regularly clean the blades. This procedure also works well for leg wraps.

A Shower in the Stable

When I used to hose down my horses, the water went everywhere and ended up creating a layer of mud on the ground. It wasn't very practical: the horses got all dirty and so did I. So I decided to install a horse shower on one side of the stable. It's not complicated to make a horse shower for your stable if you're handy with tools.

Here's how I did it:

1. First, I laid some slabs to make a deck. Then I poured 200 lb (90 kg) of concrete into a Styrofoam cooler to create a base for the shower. I used bricks to create four feet to raise the base and make room for the water intake pipe.

2. I used three rigid tubes for the shower because I wanted to be able to take it apart. I inserted the first round tube (with a diameter larger than a garden hose) through the concrete base. Note: this step must be done when the concrete is still wet. Next, I overlapped a square tube around it. The shower must be at least 6 feet (2 m) high so the horse can easily move underneath it.

3. For the next step, I fit a second round tube inside the top of the square tube. This round tube must be bent at both ends. The joints between the three tubes are made with two washers, each welded to a tube to allow the shower to swivel.

4. Then I slid a good quality garden hose inside the tubes and let it stick out by about a yard (1 m).

5. I connected the water intake and hooked up the hand shower to finish the project. Wait for everything to cool before painting your horse shower.

If you're not so handy, you can buy PVC hoses (like those used to drain water from a sink) from a hardware store. These hoses fit inside each other and are rigid; moreover, the connectors and bends are easily adapted and stick together with a special glue.

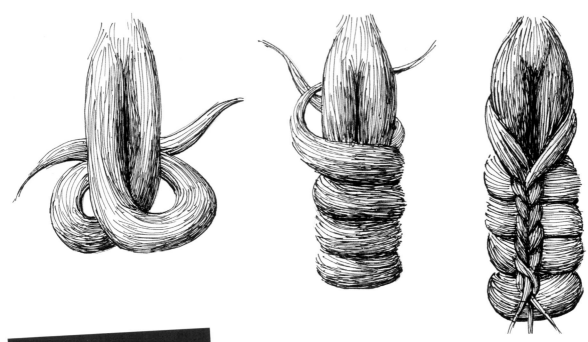

Long Tail Short Tail

In my riding center, we tie up our horses' tails when they get worked on muddy ground so they don't get needlessly dirty.

Our way of braiding their tails is both quick and easy. Here how we do it: First, separate the hairs on the horse's tail in two sections from the dock. Lift the right section while turning it clockwise around the dock. Repeat with the left section but in a counter-clockwise direction. Divide the ends of both sections into three and make a traditional braid. The end of the braid can either be kept visible or hidden.

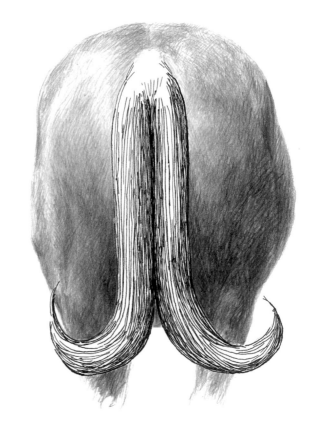

Watch Out for Flying Hooves!

My horse is pretty ticklish during grooming and unfortunately he is quick to kick. I must be very careful to avoid getting kicked and the situation gets aggravated when I need to give him a treatment. I found an easy way to prevent him from kicking: I firmly lift his dock or the rigid part of his tail. The coccygeal vertebrae at the top of the tail are an extension of the spine and the horse is very sensitive to this action that reverberates throughout his whole body. I get someone to hold my horse's tail when I need to treat him or take care of his hind legs and hold it myself when I brush his hindquarters. This method is easier and less dangerous than holding him by the foreleg. When you lift one of your horse's legs, the position becomes risky if the horse puts all of his weight on that leg or if he brusquely jerks his front leg away.

MAJOR CLEAN-UP

Seeing how dirty my horse's nylon halter, lunge and cotton girth were, I needed to take drastic measures! But in winter, it's not practical to hose this equipment down with water in the stable. So I put everything in my cloth grooming bag, close it up tight and throw it in the washing machine. I get amazing results and my grooming bag gets a good cleaning too!

GREASING WITHOUT THE MESS

In winter, my horse's hooves get weakened by moisture in the air. Used occasionally, Stockholm tar works wonders on the horn on your horse's hooves. However, this product is quite dirty and leaves stains on your skin that can't be removed by simply washing with soap and water. Not to be deterred, I found a way to make the stains disappear. I gently rub my skin with a piece of cotton soaked in 70 percent modified alcohol. The stain and odor are gone and there's no damage to my skin.

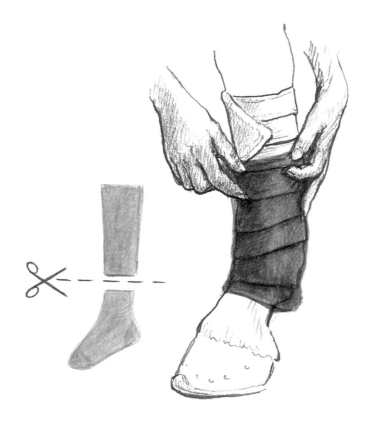

Legs of a Star

My horse has the annoying tendency to eat his stable wraps when he's in his stall. I have tried many times to break him of this bad habit, but to no avail. I finally got him to stop by covering each wrap with a knee-high stocking with the foot cut off. The horse doesn't like the feel of the nylon material on his lips because it gives off a small discharge of static electricity. When his leg wraps are covered with the nylon stocking, he no longer wants to bite them.

SALAD OIL FOR PROTECTION

When the weather turns rainy, my horses in the pasture often fall victim to mud fever. To treat this condition, I rub their legs from hoof to knee with salad oil. The water and mud slide off their hair and won't penetrate their skin, which gives them time to heal even in muddy conditions.

GENTLE GROOMING

I leave my horse in the pasture all year long. He loves it, but grooming becomes more complicated in the winter. Even a good combing and brushing can't get rid of the little balls of soil that get stuck to his hair, especially in delicate areas like his withers, lower limbs or head. I found a very effective solution to fix this: I use a fine-toothed lice comb to gently remove the rest of the dried soil where the curry comb can't reach. This way, his coat is freed of dirt and he appreciates the special attention.

TAME THAT TOUSLE!

During the summer, my horse constantly rubs his dock against the trees in his paddock, which results in a cauliflower-shaped tousle at the base of his tail. It's not very elegant when we attend shows. The only way I have found to fix this irritation is by greasing it. At the first sign of this behavior, I apply a thin layer of lard at the base of his tail. My horse stops scratching immediately and he's much more presentable during competitions!

 # Natural Hair Spray

My horse's mane falls in every direction on both sides of his neck. It's hard to get it to stay nice and smooth on one side of his neck. To fix this, I dissolve some sugar in a glass of water and soak his mane hairs with it. I sometimes braid the hairs on one side of his neck to "coax" them into keeping the look I want. My horse finally looks stylish!

19

Lift That Hoof

As part of the breaking-in regimen of my 1-year-old colt, I'm training him to lift his feet. He doesn't really understand what I'm asking of him and panics when I ask him to lift his back feet. To desensitize him, I use a bamboo rod mounted with a glove in the shape of a hand. Holding the bamboo rod at arm's length, I brush the glove against him from his croup to his fetlock. This way I can stay out of his reach without bending over. My horse doesn't feel stressed or "threatened" when I approach him and I'm not a risk of getting kicked. In general, my horses quickly become less ticklish and I can lift their feet without distressing them.

BRAIDING LESSON

My mare has very long beautiful hair, but her mane is hard to untangle. I found an original and elegant way to braid it: I start the braid with three strands at the top of the mane, then each time I take the top strand, I add in more hair from the next strand. I finish with a classic braid and tie it with an elastic. This type of braid stays in place for 2 to 4 weeks. It's easy to undo and you get a nice wavy effect when you take it out.

Soak Your Hay

Horses that cough need hay that has been wet thoroughly. Regular wheelbarrows are not ideal because you can't drain water from them and the extra weight of the water makes it difficult to distribute the hay. However, you can adapt your wheelbarrow for this task using a 4 ½ inch (12 cm) long drain pipe (1 ½ inches or 40 mm in diameter), a screw cap and an assembly sleeve of the same diameter. Drill a 1 ½ inch (40 mm) diameter hole in the bottom of your wheelbarrow. Glue the assembly sleeve in the hole. Wait a bit, then install the drain pipe and attach a small chain to the screw cap so you won't lose it. Now all you need to do is fill your wheelbarrow with hay and water. After soaking the hay, unscrew the cap to drain the water. Two-wheeled wheelbarrows work well because they are easy to empty.

BRUSH YOUR BIT

In my riding club, I noticed that some people just didn't clean their bits, whether through negligence or laziness, without really understanding why it's important to do so. Children in particular were likely to neglect this task because they found it to be a dirty chore. To encourage good hygiene, I made used toothbrushes available to my fellow riders. At first the kids found this funny, but now they clean their bits. For hygienic reasons, use one toothbrush per horse.

Sugary Bit

When I bought my horse, nothing could convince him to take the bit. I tried everything . . . and then I found a trick that worked!

Some horses find the steel bit too cold, so you need to warm it up in your hands. But this still wasn't enough of an incentive for my horse. So I smeared some honey on the mouthpiece and now there's no problem! My horse has such a sweet tooth that he opens right up!

YOU CAN'T CATCH FLIES WITH VINEGAR . . .

During the summer, flies and other insects bother not only horses, but also their human companions. I have discovered a super-effective insect repellent: I half fill a spray bottle (an old conditioner bottle does the trick) with white vinegar and top it up with water. I spray this everywhere on my horse's body, especially his mane and tail. Not only is the vinegar non-allergenic, but it protects just as well as regular bug repellent. And it costs next to nothing!

NATURAL GLOSS

My mare's coat sometimes gets dull. I don't like using hair polish products sold in saddler's stores because I find them too "chemical."

When a good grooming isn't enough to make my mare's coat shine, I use this simple and natural trick to brighten her coat: I rub a handful of damp hay (not wet!) all over her body.

Then all I need to do is dust her off and my mare's coat is beautiful, shiny and bright.

Spring Cleaning

When the weather is nice, I like to give my grooming brushes a good cleaning. I empty my grooming bag into a basin or sink filled with warm water and detergent and let everything soak for a few minutes. Then I rinse the items with water and let them dry on a window ledge or damp towel. Instead of detergent, I sometimes use bleach to disinfect my equipment, especially if my horse has had parasites or mites. When I do that, it's important to rinse thoroughly to get the bleach out. It's so much nicer to use equipment when it's good and clean!

Sensitive Ears

I bought an adorable leisure horse to go horseback riding, but unfortunately, he can't stand getting his ears touched. This is a real problem when trying to get him to wear his headstall and browband.

Rather than fight with him and lose his trust, I invented a new bridle system. I removed the browband and installed two snaps on the cheek pieces connected to the bit. I gently place the headstall on the nape of his neck behind his ears without touching them and then put the bit in his mouth. Then I attach the bit to the snaps on the cheek pieces. I attach the throatlatch and we're done! My horse doesn't get stressed and we can enjoy a peaceful ride.

PEACEFUL GROOMING

Like any self-respecting purebred, my mare is pretty ticklish. When I groom her, she twists in every direction and turns from side to side. It's a real challenge! Although I know she's gentle and won't try to kick me, she has managed to pin me against the wall of her stall even when tied.

Since my stable has two rows of stalls across from each other, I decided to cross-tie my mare using two lunges strung between two stalls. I attached snaps to the rings on the halter and hooked the lunges up on either side of the bars in the stalls at a height of about 6 feet (2 m). This way, I can curry-comb and brush my mare in peace!

BEAT THE HEAT

When I compete in the heat of summer, I place a large garbage can full of water in each stall. That way, the horses always have access to water and I don't need to continually fill their water buckets.

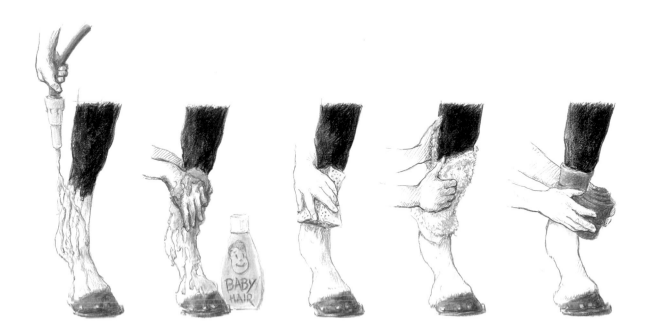

 # Whiter than White

White stockings are very pretty, but it's not always easy to keep them perfectly white, especially with the show season starting in March when the show grounds are still pretty muddy (not to mention the manure and urine stains on my horse's legs if the stalls aren't very clean.)

Here's my tip for whitening my horse's leg markings the day before a show. I vigorously scrub his lower limbs with baby shampoo and rinse them off completely with water, repeating as necessary to remove all traces of suds. After sponging off his legs and rubbing them with a towel, I wait until they are completely dry before applying blue leg wraps to the white stockings to keep them clean. It's a trick I learned from my grandmother who used little blue balls to keep her white linen from turning yellow.

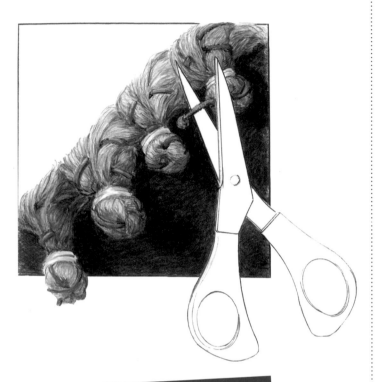

Mane Extensions

This summer, my mare scratched herself so much that she made holes in her mane, which isn't very practical for making button braids, especially since the regrowth sticks out everywhere. This happens quite often since she's very sensitive to insect bites and takes her revenge by scratching. So I got into the habit of thickening her plaits with bits of wool of the same color as her mane where the hairs are shorter. I add them directly to the braid before rolling the button on her neck. You can't tell the difference. I tuck in any stray tufts and hold them in place with a bit of gel or sweetened water. My mare's mane looks great!

STAIN PROTECTION

Gray horses are the hardest to keep clean. It's not unusual for them to get their tail dirty in the horse trailer when traveling to a show. I found a way to protect my horse's tail using an old pair of leggings or pantyhose.
1. I cut off the feet of the pantyhose and pass my hand through the leg like a bracelet.
2. With the same hand, I grab my horse's tail at the base of his spine and with my other hand, I pull his tail through the pantyhose like I would for a scrunchie or an elastic.
3. I stretch the pantyhose along the entire length of his tail and secure it to the top of the tail wrap for the duration of the trip.
4. When we arrive, my horse's tail is clean and not tangled.

WATER SUPPLY

I haven't had a chance yet to hook up running water to my horse's stall. Filling garbage cans full of water and hauling them to the stall was not a permanent solution. So I attached a haynet to the wall at a height of 4 feet (1.2 m) and placed a 5 gallon (20 l) jug inside. I then connected the jug to the drinking trough with a water pipe. I also made a hole on top of the jug so it can be filled with a funnel.

NEW LIFE FOR AN OLD LOCKER

My emphysemic horses couldn't tolerate dust in their hay. Instead, they tended to trample it in the mud and use it as bedding.

I checked my local supermarket to see if I could find an old shopping cart to store the hay. Sympathetic to my plight, the boss let me have an old storage locker that was even bigger than a cart. Now, the hay stays clean and my horses eat it dust-free because when it falls on the floor, it stays under the locker and out of their reach.

Squeaky-Clean to the Tip of Her Nose

My mare couldn't stand getting her head wet, so shower time turned into a real chore. Of course, she takes great delight in rolling in the mud as soon as I turn her into the pasture!

My solution is to use an old washcloth. After showering her body and brushing her head to get most of the dirt off, I use a damp washcloth to finish washing her head.

It took a while for her to get used to it, especially around the ears, but she has gradually accepted this "ritual" and now associates it with a caress.

DUST CONTROL

When I clean my stable, the slightest sweep of the broom or duster raises a cloud of dust that gets in my eyes and nose and settles on my glasses. Over the long term, exposure to dust can lead to breathing problems, colds or allergies. So to control the dust, I spray the stable with a garden sprinkler to create a fine mist. The result is astounding! I can sweep without worrying about the dust because it stays on the ground.

A Shiny Dark Coat

To get a dark horse's coat to shine, I use a microfiber cleaning glove like the ones that you'd use to clean your car's dashboard. It's softer than a brush, so it's great for horses who don't like their head to be touched. What's more, the dust is gone. For a finishing touch, I soak it in household white vinegar and rub it all over my horse. His coat just sparkles!

SOAP IN A BOTTLE

To clean leather with glycerin saddle soap, instead of getting a bucket of water and endlessly rubbing the bar of soap with a damp sponge, I cut up little pieces of saddle soap and add them to an old bottle of window-washer that had been thoroughly cleaned and rinsed. I fill the bottle with water and shake to dissolve the soap pieces. All I need to do is spray my leather with the nozzle and rub with a sponge.

Quick Drying

After being worked, when my horse is wet and it's too cold for a shower, I fill a bucket with hot water and a bit of 70 percent modified alcohol. Since the alcohol makes the water evaporate more quickly, I soak my sponge and rub it all over my horse's body. I finish by rubbing his coat with the sweat scraper and he's dry in no time!

Shoulder Protection

I invented an alternative to a shoulder guard that is easier to slip on. I cut an old stable shirt and added fluffy fabric to the areas most likely to rub against my horse's hair. You can either remove the breast straps and sew both parts or keep the breast straps in place. One of the belly straps was also moved after also being "fluffed up." And there you have it, no more blanket chafing!

In fact, I stopped using a shoulder guard entirely. Instead, I sewed an old carpet on the inside of my horse's blanket at shoulder height to serve as a lining.

Best Practices for Clipping Your Horse

I'm not very talented when it comes to clipping my horse and have trouble creating an outline with chalk. As a result, my horse often has a "punk rock" look! So I tried a different approach.

I saddle my horse without his saddle pad. After walking a few minutes to get the hairs to settle in place, I can see a clear imprint of the saddle where the hairs are slightly flattened and I trace the outline of the saddle with chalk. It's very easy for me to see this and all I have to do is clip around it.

 # Comfort and Safety

When I saddle and bridle my riding club horse, I never know where to put his reins so he won't trample them while waiting to leave his stall. I don't like threading them through the stirrup because when the horse lowers his head to nibble some straw, he gets jerked in the mouth. So I twist the reins a bit and hold them in place with the throatlatch. The horse can then lower his head comfortably and safely, without walking on his reins. Never let your reins drag on the ground!

A PRACTICAL APRON

When I need to style and braid a horse's mane or tail, I wear an apron with a large front pocket to hold all the equipment I'll need: elastics, comb, brush and a clothes pin to keep the braid in place if I get interrupted in the middle of the job.

TIME OFF MY SADDLE

When the rainy season comes, I trade my leather saddle for a synthetic one. I used to be reluctant to store my leather saddle for months without using it for fear that it would get wet and become damaged. A saddler friend gave me great advice. I carefully clean my leather saddle and rub it with oil using a clean rag. I put it on a saddle rack and cover it up with a protective blanket. If there's any mold on the saddle when I want to reuse it, I just clean it with glycerin saddle soap and it's as clean as a whistle! You can do the same thing with your bridles.

A Horse Vacuum!

My horse goes to the paddock every day. His chestnut coat gets so full of dust that he starts to look gray. So I recycled my old vacuum and added a curtain brush attachment at the end of the hose. I got my horse used to the noise and now I brush him with the vacuum all over his body. I do this in his stall, but for horses that are a bit nervous, the grooming area would be ideal.

BOOST YOUR CONDITIONER

To make your conditioner even more effective, let it dry after you spray it on your horse's mane and tail. I spray my horse as soon as he enters the stable, then I take my time preparing what I need to settle into a long grooming session. As a result, all it takes is a few strokes of the comb to untangle my horse's mane and tail!

A SHINY COAT

My mare's coat is a dust magnet. The more I brush her, the dustier she gets. I have a simple little trick to get her coat to shine. At the end of a grooming session, I take a handful of hay from the feed bag, dip it in water and rub it all over her coat. Then all I do is dust her off; her coat is shiny without being slippery. This is inexpensive and environmentally friendly!

 # Fail-Safe Hairstyle

How many times have I found my horse completely disheveled on the morning of a show, his button braids undone and straw sticking out of his mane, looking rather pleased with himself? Even though I took great pains to carefully braid his mane the day before (to avoid putting any undue stress on him right before the show), his button braids that were wound nice and tight and fixed in place with hairspray didn't survive his nighttime rolling.

But I found the perfect solution: I cut a pair of pantyhose lengthwise in two. I gently cover the pretty rosettes in my horse's mane with the cut pantyhose and hold it in place with an elastic on each button. It's as easy as that! The next morning, my horse is presentable and ready for the show.

Poster Distraction

During the winter, my horses spend a lot more time in their stall. Since I worry that they'll get bored, I found a simple solution to keep them occupied.

A study on animal behavior showed that a life-sized poster of a fellow horse helped relieve boredom. Horses in the study stared longer at a horse poster than at any other images. This is a simple twist on hanging a mirror in their living quarters, which can be hard to install safely in a stall.

ALWAYS LOOKING HIS BEST

I like to see my horse with a gorgeous mane and tail. However, brushing alone isn't enough to smooth out his tangled hairs, which are often mixed with bits of straw. Conditioners sold in saddler's stores are effective but expensive. So I tried using my own cream rinse that I transferred to a spray bottle and diluted with water. It works like a charm! My horse's mane and tail are now easy to brush.

RECYCLED CLIPPINGS

I found a way to recycle the horse hairs that I collect after a clipping.

One year, I decided to salvage the clippings. In the spring, I placed them in a mesh bag like the ones used to hold lemons and hung the bag in a tree. Birds came to peck at the mesh and used the hairs to build their nests.

What a green idea!

Tail Protection

Even with a tail wrap, my horse tends to injure the top of his tail when he travels in the horse trailer. I tried the conventional method of wrapping a polo bandage around his tail under the tail wrap, but this created tiny injuries that took a long time to heal. Finally, I applied a self-stick bandage like the kind that people use for a sprain to the base of my horse's tail before protecting it with the tail wrap during transportation. It adheres perfectly without any unwanted chafing. Now we can head off to the show with peace of mind.

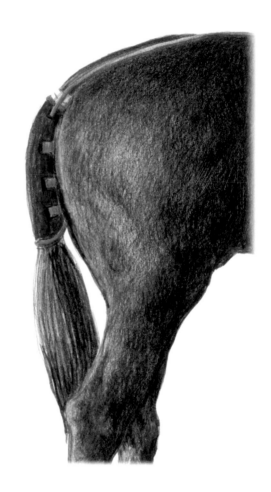

HAY SHOWER

Hauling a watering can or having to roll and unroll the hose to soak my hay was inconvenient and time-consuming. That prompted me to invent a hand shower system that I installed directly in the stall close to where I put the hay for my horse. I connected the hand shower to the water intake in the watering trough and hung a metal box for storage. Now I can control the exact amount of water that I add to my hay. And everything is right at my fingertips!

A Summer Trim

Since I'm not very clever with my hands, I'm not very good at thinning out my horse's mane. My horse hates it and won't stop fidgeting, which doesn't help! To avoid making holes in his mane or giving him a geometric haircut, I trim his hair with a disposable razor strand by strand like a comb. This is an easier way to thin his mane and achieve a consistent length. You can't tell the difference, I save time and my horse is much calmer.

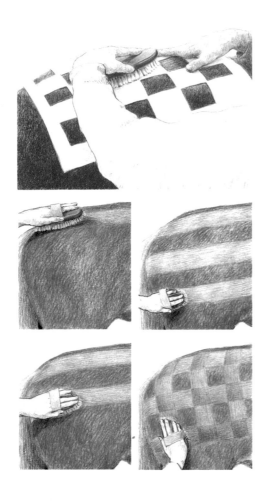

Checkerboard

An Artistic Touch

I find a checkerboard pattern drawn on a horse's croup really striking, especially on a bright coat. I wanted to master this technique and decorate my horse's croup myself.

There are two ways of achieving a checkerboard design. You can simply brush your horse's hair against the grain in a crisscross pattern on his croup, or you can get a flexible stencil in a checkered pattern from a saddler's store. All you need to do is lay the stencil on your horse's croup and brush the hair against the grain to show off the squares. When you've finished, wet the decorated area with sweetened water or beer to get the hair to stay in place and make it shine.

A PERFECT COAT

I have two adorable fillies. It's important to get them used to being groomed, so I brush them regularly. However, even after a good brushing, I still find dead hairs stuck to their coat. I use a lint roller to finish the job. The unwanted hair and dirt stick to the adhesive roller and my fillies' coats are perfectly clean. I just remove the sticky tape and put the roller away in my grooming kit until the next time!

Quick Foot Wash

It often rains during the spring and when I go horseback riding, my horse's hooves get covered in sticky mud well before we're ready to come home. If water is in short supply, I place my horse's foot in a bucket and pour just enough water inside to wet his foot and rub the mud off with a brush. Then I can pick his feet like I normally would. Of course, this technique is only possible with a docile horse!

WHAT BEAUTIFUL EYES YOU HAVE

I found that it wasn't very practical to use a wet sponge to clean the dried discharge in the corner of my horse's eyes. He didn't like the feeling of water seeping into his eyes. So I found a great solution: I use moisturizing makeup remover wipes. The dirt sticks to the wipes; it's quick and easy and my horse seems to like it!

ESSENTIAL TIPS

CARE

Stuffed Carrot Surprise!

Instead of regular horse treats, I concocted this recipe for a stuffed carrot surprise.

Ingredients

A carrot, some grass and hay, a few pellets of feed and some liquid honey.

Directions

Cut the carrot in two with a knife and empty out the middle. Fill the hollow in each half with hay and pellets. Stick both pieces back together with a dollop of honey. Your horse's treat is ready to serve!

TIPS FOR STORING FOOD

I'm fortunate to be able to keep my horse with me at home, but this means that I've had to improvise to avoid acquiring a whole range of gear that horse professionals use. For example, to protect my grain and horse feed from moisture and rodents, I store them in 11 gallon (50 l) plastic garbage cans. I use a 1 quart (1 l) tin can to measure feed rations. Here's another thrifty tip: I salvage "downgraded" apples (that can't be sold because of their appearance) from a local farmer. He's happy to give me two or three crates for my horse. It helps to be neighborly when your neighbor's a farmer!

Flaked Cookies

Ingredients

A cup of flour, a cup of rolled oats, a cup of grated carrots, half a cup of honey, 3 tablespoons of water, 2 tablespoons of oil, a teaspoon of salt and a bit of butter to grease the baking sheet.

Directions

Mix all ingredients until dough is smooth. Using two teaspoons, shape the dough into little balls and drop them onto a buttered cookie sheet, leaving a large space between each. Flatten each ball of dough with a floured spoon and cook in a 350°F (180°C) oven for 15 minutes. The cookies are ready when they are golden brown in color.

🐴 Dinner Time!

The riding club has a large trunk to store feed pellets. We put our heads together and found this inexpensive solution for easily distributing feed rations to the 15 horses in the stable. We use a wheeled garbage can to haul their food. The wheels make it easy to roll in the stables and bear most of the weight. Now it's simple and convenient to feed our 15 horses!

Good Quality Hay

In September, it's time to replenish hay supplies for the winter. It's especially important to ensure good storage conditions, as hay loses its energy value easily if it's not kept in a dry, well-ventilated area. Too much moisture will make hay go moldy, but too little moisture will make it brittle and give off a fine dust that can cause respiratory disorders in horses. To keep your hay at an optimal moisture level, sprinkle coarse salt between the layers as you stack the bales of hay. The horses appreciate the salty taste and the hay will always be palatable!

A SPECIAL SNACK

I wanted to prepare a special snack for my horse. So I salvaged a day-old hollowed-out bread bowl at the bakery that I let dry until it was nice and hard, then filled it with cut carrots. My horse just loved this snack in its edible bowl!

If you give this snack to your horse, stay with him while he's eating to make sure he doesn't bite off chunks of bread that are too large to swallow.

Surprise Filling

My horse hates taking medication, especially any that comes in powdered form like anti-inflammatory drugs. To make this process easier, I heat a cream-filled snack cake (such as Twinkies) for a few seconds in the microwave to soften the filling. I open it in two, sprinkle powder on the filling and close it back up. When the snack cake has cooled, the powder is hidden inside the filling. Now I just give this special "treat" to my horse, who doesn't suspect a thing. His sweet tooth gets the better of him and I can administer his medication without any waste!

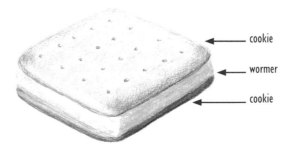

cookie

wormer

cookie

COMFORTABLE HEADSTALL

My horse's sensitive skin is easily irritated by the rubbing of the buckles on his cheek piece, especially when he falls prey to insect bites. To make him more comfortable and avoid inflammation, I use this simple trick: I slide a bicycle inner tube on his headstall long enough to cover the buckles on both cheek pieces. The rubber protects his skin from the rough spots on his bridle.

Don't Lie Down

I found a way to get horses to stop lying down like a cow, a position that can cause injury to their elbows. This is a solution that I have successfully tested on my mare. All you need is five old tennis balls and a 15 to 20 inch (40–50 cm) strip of leather. Make a hole on both sides of the tennis balls and string them together on the strip of leather to make a lovely pastern bracelet for your horse that he can wear whenever he's in his stall.

NEW USE FOR DIAPER RASH CREAM

All year long, my two mares get bitten by midges until they bleed, especially around the ears and under the belly. Now, I apply a diaper rash cream once or twice a week. The ointment heals their skin and also repels midges. It's not pretty, but it works!

Hens to the Rescue

Every summer, my Provence donkey would have to endure fly and horsefly bites. But that all stopped when I acquired two laying hens. The hens spent the summer under the donkey's belly, busily pecking at insects that came to harass him. Thanks to these small and nimble "fly catchers," my donkey now spends his summers in peace without needing any insect repellent.

Stuffed Apple or Carrot

My horse needs to take regular medication in the form of capsules prescribed by my veterinarian, but he refuses to take them! So I found a simple but effective solution: I empty out the middle of a carrot or apple with a potato peeler or an apple corer and hide the capsule inside. Then I plug the hole and give the treat to my horse, who doesn't suspect a thing!

Puree on the Menu

My horse has a voracious appetite and bolts down his food with vigorous shakes of his head. Not only does he scatter half his ration in the straw, but when he eats too fast he has trouble digesting. So I moisten his food with warm water each time I feed him. The compact puree is hard to spill and forces him to eat more slowly. If your horse needs to take medication, you can add it to the puree and he won't even tell the difference. Since I've started this, my horse doesn't gobble his food anymore and his digestion has improved.

DIY GRAZING MUZZLE

I put my horse to pasture when the weather gets nice, and since he's a first-rate glutton, he tends to get a bit colicky. I needed a grazing muzzle to keep him from eating. While waiting to purchase one, I used a big, empty plastic container large enough to fit my horse's head. Using a cutter, I made two breathing holes in the bottom of the container the size of his nostrils and two slits near the top to thread some baler twine through. I hooked up this contraption to the halter rings on either side of my horse's head. And there you have the perfect DIY grazing muzzle.

Snack Time

I like to personally prepare treats for my pony with all his favorite ingredients. Try these cookies (but in moderation, of course!)

Ingredients

A cup of flour, a cup of rolled oats, carrots or chopped apples, a cup of honey or molasses, 3 tablespoons of water, 2 tablespoons of oil, a teaspoon of salt and a pat of butter.

Directions

Mix all ingredients except the butter until dough is smooth. Using two teaspoons, shape the dough into little balls and drop them onto a buttered cookie sheet, leaving a large space between each. Flatten each ball of dough with a floured spoon and cook in a 350°F (180°C) oven for 15 minutes. The cookies are ready when they are golden brown in color.

Edible Wreath

I like to keep things interesting when it comes to my horse's treats, so during the festive season, I made him a wreath.

Ingredients

Hay, soft straw, a small bunch of carrots and four or five apples.

1. Make a long braid with the hay.
2. Wrap bits of straw around the braid about every 10 cm (4 inches) to reinforce the wreath.
3. Cut the apples and carrots into chunks.
4. Wedge the apple and carrot chunks into the wreath or, for a sturdier hold, make a hole in the middle and string them on a strand of hay like you would for a string of pearls. Snack time!

Birch to Nibble On

My horse needs to nibble when he's in his stall and he was in the habit of attacking his straw after wolfing down his hay. Now that I use shavings for his bedding, I've added a birch log to his stall. Birch is a soft wood so he can sink his teeth into it. It relieves his stress and he leaves his stall door alone.

Natural Fly Repellent

Since I live in the country, I've learned a trick or two for keeping flies away from my stable. I plant basil, pennyroyal and French marigold, plants known for their insect-repellent properties, in flower baskets. I place the baskets at the entrance to the stable (out of reach of the horses, just to be on the safe side). Geraniums are also a good choice.

Here's another old household remedy to keep the bugs away: cut an onion or a lemon in two and pick it with cloves. It's very effective at the club house and it smells great!

Pennyroyal

Basil

Marigold

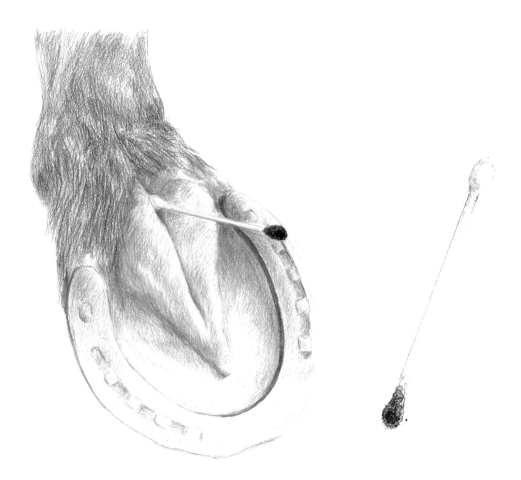

HOMEMADE HANGING BALL

Even though my horse has a neighbor in the stall right next to his, he sometimes appears to get bored. Horse toys sold in saddler's store can be expensive, but the idea is usually simple and easy to replicate. So I decided to make a hanging ball for my horse's stall. I placed a beach ball inside a haynet and hung it from the ceiling at the same height as my horse's head. Now he can have fun batting it around.

Multipurpose Cotton Swabs

Horses with tight heels often have problems with their frogs. Tar is a great way to treat this, but it is hard to apply on horses with deep clefts. Using cotton swabs is a simple and hygienic solution. One end can be used to clean the frog and the other to apply the tar.

50

NO-BAKE CAKE

You need two carrots, one apple, a handful of feed pellets or beet pulp and a tablespoon of honey. Cut the apple and carrots into small pieces and soak the pellets or beet pulp in warm water for 2 minutes. Mix everything in a small bowl and add a spoonful of liquid honey. Cover and refrigerate overnight. The next day, take the "cake" out of the bowl and add it to your horse's bucket. It's a real treat!

CARROT CAKE

Grate a few carrots, add some honey to make it all stick together and mix well to give this cake a nice shape.

WORMING WITH HONEY

My pony refused to take her wormer so I thought it would be a good idea to mask the taste with honey. I mixed the medicine with honey and spread it on a piece of hard bread. My pony thought it was a treat and gobbled it down. With this approach, you can customize the ingredients to suit your horse's tastes.

Stuffed Apple

Ingredients

One apple, half a grated carrot, some corn flakes, liquid honey.

Directions

Cut the apple in two and empty out each half. Mix the grated carrot, corn flakes and a bit of honey in a bowl.

Fill both cavities of the apple with stuffing and spread a bit of honey around the edges so both halves stick together.

Note: Any combination of ingredients can be mixed with honey to make the stuffing. Here are some ideas: banana and granola, carrot and rolled oats, peanut butter and corn flakes, or applesauce, peppermints and flaked feed.

Now all you need to do is treat your horse!

An Endless Supply of Toys

My horse spends a lot of time in the paddock and enjoys taking in everything that goes on around him, and when he's brought to his stall, he tends to get bored. I had to provide some kind of entertainment so he wouldn't destroy his feeding trough and stall. My grown-up children left their old things behind when they moved out. So I reclaimed several toys for my horse: a rattle, a stuffed toy that I use to hide a carrot and a tennis ball filled with sand. I hang one of them in his stall and change toys every couple of days so he doesn't tire of the game. It's an inventive way to arouse his curiosity.

I'm the new toy*

*still 2 days left to live ...

HANGING CARROTS

To entertain and treat my horse when he's in his stall, I rigged up a "carrot attraction" using some baler twine, a horseshoe nail (clean, of course), some carrot or apple chunks and a knife. Cut some carrots or apples into thick chunks. Make a hole in them with the horseshoe nail so you can thread them on the twine, like a string of pearls. Using a piece of twine about 1 ½ yards (1.5 m) long, make a knot at one end and thread a piece of carrot or apple onto it until it reaches the knot. Make a knot on the other side of the carrot or apple so it stays put and repeat until the string is full. You will soon have a pretty garland to hang over the door of your horse's stall! Don't forget to remove the twine once your horse has finished eating his treat.

Weaving Horse

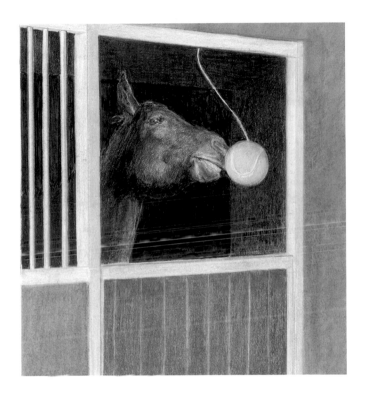

To relieve boredom, my horse would sway from side to side at his stall door for hours on end. This stable vice is known as weaving. To make matters worse, the other horses in the stable started to mimic him! I quickly had to put a stop to this. Rather than install a yoke door grill to prevent him from swaying, I decided to try a more playful solution. I hung a tennis ball at the end of a string in the middle of the opening of his stall door. Although at first he was surprised by the ball, now it's my horse's favorite toy!

SAY NO TO BOREDOM

My horse lives in his stall and I'm afraid he'll get bored during the day since I can only spend time with him in the evening.

He's a real glutton and quickly devours his rations, so I can't say that mealtime occupies a large part of his day! His hay, which he gets in the morning and afternoon, quickly disappears and only offers a brief distraction. Even a ball hung in his stall was just a passing fancy. After giving it some thought, I made him a "feed box." I recycled a plastic jug and made large holes in it. I poured some feed pellets inside, closed the lid tightly and left the jug in his stall. To get to his ration, my hungry horse has to push and roll the jug around with his nose to get the food to come out. This little game keeps him occupied for part of the day and I'm sure he won't lose interest in it! Not to mention that eating more slowly is undoubtedly better for his health.

Drink without Rushing

My horse perspires easily when he's at work. When I bring him back to the stall, he's often soaking wet and very thirsty. He'd readily gulp down half a gallon of cold water, but this could lead to colic. Given his strength and size, I have a hard time holding him back.
So to force him to lift his head from his water bucket, I follow this technique: I let him drink a few sips, then I slide my finger into the corner of his mouth to let some air in. It's a good way to get him to take a breather! Then I pull his head toward me, slip a halter on and walk him to dry him off a bit before letting him drink some more.

Leaving the bridle on your horse when you bring him to his stall is also a good solution. His bit will prevent him from drinking too quickly.

How to Get Your Horse to Drink

During a competition, riders will tell you that their horses may lose their bearings and have difficulty drinking. As a former endurance rider, I know that this situation can have some serious consequences. When I competed, I started a little ritual at least 10 days before the race. I placed pieces of apples and carrots in a light-colored bucket and gave them to my horse as a snack. The next day, I added two fingers of water to the bucket before giving my horse his treat. After a few days, I increased the amount of water to force him to drink before eating the apples and carrots. On the day of the race, I used the same bucket and water brought from home (stored in a jug) so as not to disturb his habits. This way I was able to condition my horse and had no trouble getting him to drink almost the entire bucket!

AWAY WITH HORSE L...

During the summer, my horses ...y spending time in the pasture where they can eat fresh grass, but that also means they're plagued by horse louse flies. I found a simple and inexpensive way to protect my horses from this affliction. Using a paintbrush, I dab some cooking oil on my horses' parts where the flies are likely to land, especially the anus, vulva, penile sheath, teats and crotch. The flies avoid landing on the horses, but if they do, they get stuck in the oil and fall off. To be effective, the oil should be reapplied every 3 or 4 days. Be careful not to get kicked if your horse is ticklish.

HOMEMADE INSECT REPELLENT

I don't believe in commercial insect repellents available on the market. My insect repellent tip is cheap and environmentally friendly. I apply vinegar to my mare's coat every day with a damp sponge to protect her during bug season, taking care to avoid the mucus membrane areas. It's not 100 percent effective, but it offers some relief.

NO MORE FLEAS

When it's time to wash my horse's saddlecloth and other blankets, I pile them on the floor in the laundry room. A couple of months ago, my dog started sleeping on the pile of horse blankets. Ever since then, I've noticed that his fleas are gone! Apparently, the horse smell keeps these nasty insects away. Now I know what to use to line my dog's bed! But of course, this doesn't replace his regular tick and flea treatment.

STOP CHEWING!

My horse chews on his lunge. To get him to stop, I covered the lunge with a piece of garden hose cut to the right length. The lunge is protected by the hose and is no longer damaged by my horse's teeth!

An Elegant Flyswatter

My mare doesn't have a very thick forelock and that means her sensitive eyes are at the mercy of flies. Last summer, I invented a flyswatter for her. I braided hair extensions into her forelocks with synthetic hair. It's safer than leaving her with a halter fitted with a flyswatter that can get caught somewhere.

You can add as many strands as you want. If the braids are done well, they can last up to 2 months. Synthetic hair is sold at the hairdresser's store and it's very affordable (all you need is one pack at a cost of $2 to $5 per pack). It comes in every color imaginable: blond, brown and black, but also pink, blue, yellow and red.

Here is how to braid in the synthetic hair:
1. Take a small strand of your horse's hair and a small strand of synthetic hair folded in two lengthwise.
2. Turn the folded strand of synthetic hair around your horse's hair as close to the root as possible.
3. You should have three strands in your hands: your horse's hair and two strands of synthetic hair.
4. Braid the hair tightly.
5. If you're able to, mix your horse's hair in with the synthetic hair in each of the three strands before starting to produce a more solid braid.

citronella

Homemade Mosquito Repellent

For the past year, I've been using this recipe to ward off mosquitoes that plague my horse during the summer months. Here's what you need to make 1 quart (1 l): lemongrass (citronella) leaves (available in exotic food stores), a clove of garlic (minced), vinegar, lavender essential oil and water.

1. Put the lemongrass and garlic in a salad bowl. Cover with 3 cups (700 ml) of boiling water and allow to steep overnight.

2. Filter the mixture in a strainer and add 1⅓ cups (300 ml) of vinegar and 10 drops of lavender essential oil. Now it's ready to spray on your horse's coat.

To ensure it won't cause an allergic reaction, it's best to test your potion on a small area before applying it all over your horse.

Chain Cover

My horse has the bad habit of leaning on and rubbing against the chain that bars the entrance to his stall when I leave the door open. Since he has a light gray coat, this causes nasty marks across his breast and sometimes the damage goes as deep as his skin. So to prevent him from hurting himself, I cut a piece of garden hose to cover the length of the chain. The plastic hose protects his skin from the metal chain, so he can lean all he wants. If you have a very thick chain, you can find larger hoses in aquarium stores.

A Hard Egg to Cut

We have tried many ways to remove stubborn flies' eggs that stick to the hair on our horses' limbs at the end of the summer. My grandmother brought us a special knife. It worked like a charm, but unfortunately we lost it.

Then a friend gave us some grapefruit knives, which looked a lot like our lost knife! We tried them on our horses' legs … and they did the trick! These knives are slightly curved with tiny teeth on each side and at both ends. You can buy them in kitchen stores or wherever tableware is sold.

INNER TUBE BUFFER

My old pony Apache has sensitive skin. His skin gets really irritated where his headstall rubs against it to the point where he often injures himself when he gets worked. So I made him a special buffer to alleviate his discomfort. I cut a piece of inner tube and attached it to the bridle with some tape. No more worries!

Cure for Boredom

Even though my horse spends his days in the paddock with other horses, as soon as he's in his stall, he stays close to the door and tries to get out every chance he gets. Since he's inquisitive and loves to eat, I came up with a toy to satisfy both his curiosity and his appetite. I salvaged a big plastic ball that my dog had punctured with his teeth. I made the hole a bit bigger and used a funnel to fill the ball with feed pellets. Then I placed it in my horse's feeding trough. Intrigued and amused by the rattling sound coming from the ball, he started to play with it and immediately figured out that it was a treat dispenser. He just loves it and now he's a lot less impatient when he's in his stall.

AMUSE-BOUCHE ?

For a different twist, make several holes in the ball. I don't like this option as much because the food doesn't last as long in the ball and tends to spill out into little piles, but then again, why not?

Homemade Foot Grease

I haven't always been satisfied with store-bought hoof ointments, so I decided to make a more effective product right in my own home. For this homemade recipe, carefully mix the contents of a package of henna (available in drugstores or wherever haircare products are sold) with a teaspoon of copper sulfate and some cod liver oil. Add just enough oil to get the consistency of an ointment, which can be easily brushed on. Henna has moisturizing properties, oil provides long-lasting lubrication for the hoof and copper sulfate purifies the surface of the horn. It's the perfect protection for the hoof, periople, sole and frog. Be careful when adding the copper sulfate; less is more!

DOUBLE COAT

Since my mare is clipped in the winter, I'm always afraid that she'll catch cold when I ride her, especially when we are at walk at the beginning or end of a riding session. However, bundling her up too much isn't any better, as that will make her sweat and then she'll catch cold afterwards. So when it's really cold outside, I cover her with two exercise rugs at the beginning of our training session. The first layer made of fleece goes directly on her croup followed by a second rug of thick wool. After the warm-up, I take the top layer off but leave the fleece rug in place. If my mare is really too warm, I remove the fleece layer as well when we do the exercises. This way, she always stays at "just the right temperature."

henna
Lawsonia

Copper Sulfate
Cu SO4

cod liver oil

Salt in Any Weather

My horse spends many hours a day in the pasture and I want to make sure he has access to a salt lick. During the rainy season, I found a way to protect the licking block from getting wet in the rain or dragged in the mud. I bought an 11 pound (5 kg) block and hung it from the branch of a tree in the pasture at a height accessible to my horse. To prevent the licking block from being rubbed by the twine, I slipped a piece of garden hose into the hole and inserted the twine inside the hose before attaching it to the branch. This way, the twine won't rub and cause the block to crack. I also installed a round plastic cover above the block to protect it from the rain.

Improvised Brush Holder

Stockholm tar works wonders for treating thrush. But where to put the dirty paintbrush when the job's done? The tar is so sticky that it's impossible to clean. Not to mention the hassle of getting it out from the bottom of the can when you need to use it again!

To make my life easier, I invented a holder to store the brush between uses: simply cut off the top of a small plastic bottle and tape it beside the can of tar.

KEEP TICKS AWAY

I often find ticks stuck to my horse's skin. Even though I regularly check for ticks, I'm always afraid that if I miss any my horse could be infected with piroplasmosis, a tick-borne disease. So I looked for a way to prevent ticks from attacking in the first place. I add a tablespoon of dried garlic to my horse's feed ration every day at the beginning of winter, a few months before tick season. This technique, no doubt, leaves an odor that permeates my horse's skin and keeps ticks away. But rest assured, your horse won't smell like garlic!

NO MORE SPOILED CARROTS!

When I store my mare's carrots in a bag, they tend to spoil very quickly due to moisture in the stable. This simple trick will keep them fresh longer and avoid spoilage: add some dry bread to the bag of carrots. The bread absorbs the moisture and the carrots stay fresh. However, you shouldn't leave the bread with the carrots for too long or it will become soft and wet, and eventually get moldy! You can also dry the bread out again and give it to your horse (but only if it hasn't gone moldy).

Hair Gloss to Heal Sores

Many riders encounter problems with sores that can take their mount out of commission. Depending on the location of the injury, the horse can be disabled for a long time.

When my horse had sores, I found a simple and effective solution to prevent further discomfort under his saddle and bridle. I spray the affected areas with detangling hair gloss. The tack slides more easily over the horse's coat, thus reducing the friction that causes this type of wound. You may need to add a crupper and breast plate (or breast collar), as the gloss can cause the saddle to slide forwards or backwards.

A FIX FOR MUD FEVER

My farrier gave me this simple and effective fix for mud fever. This is a homemade recipe that you can use to treat your horse's pasterns. In a bowl, mix olive oil with powdered sulfur (an animal repellent, available in drugstores). To get the right dose, add just enough sulfur to make a smooth paste. Mix well, then allow to cool and harden. This lowcost antiseptic cream can be applied liberally to your horse's affected areas. Use it well!

A Refreshing Idea

When my horses are out riding during the summer or in their stall when the weather turns hot, I use the horse's equivalent of a damp face cloth to cool them off. I take a thick sponge (available in saddler's stores), soak it in water and slide it inside the headstall. I also regularly hose down their limbs. With these cooling techniques, my horses don't suffer too much from the sweltering heat.

WASTE NOT

At feeding time, my horse rushes over to his trough and pushes his nose exuberantly through his ration of pellets, so much so that much of it falls out of his trough and into his bedding. As a result, he doesn't get his full ration or the proper nutrition.

My instructor gave me this simple trick: Place some beach pebbles in your horse's feeding trough, as long as they are large enough not be swallowed and smooth enough not to hurt him. Since the feed pellets are mixed in with the pebbles, the horse has to be more careful when eating. This forces him to eat more calmly, without rushing and without waste.

Here's another idea: I covered my horse's trough with a thick piece of stretchy fabric held in place with a strong elastic and taped on the sides to make sure the fabric stays in place. Then I cut a circular opening at the center of the trough just a bit smaller than my horse's nose. The stretchy material gives my horse access to his food but prevents it from spilling everywhere!

Stop the Spilling

My horse has a bad habit of spilling his food when he eats. He knocks his bucket with his head and often sends it flying several feet away. As a result, he doesn't eat his full ration since some of his food gets spread all over the yard. I found a simple and effective solution using an old set of reins or an old lunge. Attach one end to the handle of the bucket and the other to your horse's tie ring. This way, when he knocks his head inside the bucket, the bucket will move around but won't spill.

ODOR CONTROL

If the smell from your stable causes your neighbors to complain, use this solution to help mask the odor of urine. I line the bottom of the stall with a half-inch (1 cm) layer of flax mulch and cover it up with regular straw bedding. When the mulch turns red, it's time to change it, as it will no longer absorb the ammonia from the urine. This will improve both the look and smell of your stalls!

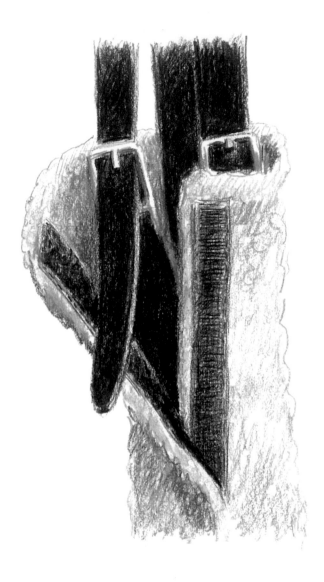

Customized Sleeve

My horse has very sensitive skin and is susceptible to girth gall, so to prevent injury I cover his girth with a synthetic sheep's skin sleeve. But now, with his new dressage saddle, the sleeve is too long and covers the buckles. It's really not practical for tightening his girth, especially when I'm mounted. So I cut about 6 inches (15 cm) along the seam of the sleeve and sewed a Velcro strip on each side. When I'm mounted, all I need to do to tighten the girth is open and close the Velcro fastener. It's easy!

OIL TO CURE CHESTNUTS

My horse has large chestnuts on his legs. I use cooking oil such as sunflower oil or olive oil available at any supermarket or even hoof grease to soften them. I apply this treatment once a week until the chestnuts fall off on their own.

Flawless Legs

In the springtime, the hair on my horse's limbs gets covered in fly eggs that are really hard to remove. I find that the easiest way to get rid of them is to simply rub them off with a pumice stone.

Another solution: I use a twin-blade disposable shaver. However, watch that your horse doesn't make any sudden movements and be careful not to shave his hair.

A Halter for Nursing Foals

My foals get used to wearing a halter at a young age, often when they are only a few weeks old. It's important to ensure that their halter doesn't rub against the mare and hurt her when she's feeding them. So I add a length of inner tube to the colts' noseband and cheek strap. The customized halter doesn't irritate the mare and the colts can suckle without hurting their mother!

Keep Your Hoof Dry

My mare had an abscess on her foot that required dressing after it was treated. The challenge was to keep the bandage clean through the rain and mud of the off-season. I protected my horse's foot with a freezer bag held in place with an elastic or some tape. The freezer bag is much sturdier than a regular plastic bag and my horse's hoof stays nice and dry.

INSECT-REPELLING ESSENTIAL OILS

I had read and heard that garlic was a great insect repellent. But it's hard to figure out how much garlic a thousand-pound (500 kg) horse would need to ingest for this treatment to be effective. Instead, I bought some garlic essential oil and added about 20 drops to a commercial bug repellent. I also make my own potion by mixing various essential oils (garlic, geranium, clove and citronella) with water. The strong smell provides the horses some relief from the bugs. Sometimes on a windy day I even get a good dose of it myself when I spray it on my mares!

 # Cure for Chapped Lips

The corners of my horse's mouth are fragile. After a cold winter, the skin around his lips gets chapped to the point where the bit might cause him injury. To prevent this, I coat his mouthpiece with sweet almond oil, a moisturizing product that has a pleasant taste. During competitions, I even wipe some oil on my horse's nostrils and lips to make them shine. Just like the thoroughbreds in an Arabian horse show, my horse looks like a star!

NO MORE SCABS

My horse sometimes gets small, dry, hard black scabs on his pastern joint or bulb. I rub some petroleum jelly on them to get rid of them. The petroleum jelly doesn't irritate his skin, which clears up nicely.

A PASTE THAT HEALS

My horse regularly gets little scabs along his neck. I concoct a paste with honey and borage oil and I find it really helps them heal.

No Hoof, No Horse

My horse used to suffer from thrush. Applying cotton balls steeped in an astringent solution like Veredus Villate on his frogs helps heal this affliction. Rather than trying to keep the cotton in place with adhesive tape that won't stick, I covered my horse's hoof with a large-sized sock! The sock protects his foot and keeps the cotton in place, so the solution has more time to act.

Pierced Bit

I had a tough time getting my horse to swallow his liquid medication. So I contrived a way to get him to take it without issue. I took an old bridle that was no longer being used and removed the noseband. I adapted a hollow stainless steel elevator bit that had a port and made a hole in the middle to allow the liquid to flow out under the horse's tongue. Then I made an opening on one of the sides of the bit and attached a little drip tube. I placed a small container above the tube and secured it to the bridle with an elastic. All that's left to do is inject the required dose into the container, adjust the drip and wait for my horse to take his medicine while calmly chewing on his bit.

THE SCENT OF TAR

My horse has the bad habit of chewing on the wooden angle posts of his shelter in the pasture. I finally found a way to get him to stop gnawing on the posts by coating them with Stockholm tar. The smell and taste of the tar deter my horse and he has stopped damaging his shelter! The tar lasts a long time so I only need to reapply it every 6 months.

HOW TO CLEAN A RUSTED BIT

When I was tidying up my tack room, I came across an old rusted bit. Aside from the rust, I thought it would be a great fit for my mare's bridle. So to clean it, I filled a small bowl with cola and let the bit soak overnight. I got amazing results without lifting a finger!

Peas to the Rescue

My horse is a bit skittish and when he panics, he sometimes bangs into things and suffers minor bumps on his limbs.

When this happens, I apply an ice pack to relieve the swelling. Since I don't keep ice in the freezer, I apply a bag of frozen peas to the affected area, which I first cover with a cotton wrap. I secure the homemade ice pack with a stable bandage and leave it on for a few minutes. That's what works best for me.

Extra tip: put the bag of peas inside another freezer bag to prevent the bandages from getting wet.

SENSITIVE TEETH

In winter, the tack room where I store my bridles is unheated, so the bits are always very cold. The feel of frozen steel against my horse's teeth and gums is very unpleasant at the beginning of a workout. So when the temperature drops, I run my horse's bit under hot water to warm it up before putting his bridle on. If you don't have access to a sink, you can always warm the bit in your hands for a few minutes. Your horse will love you for it!

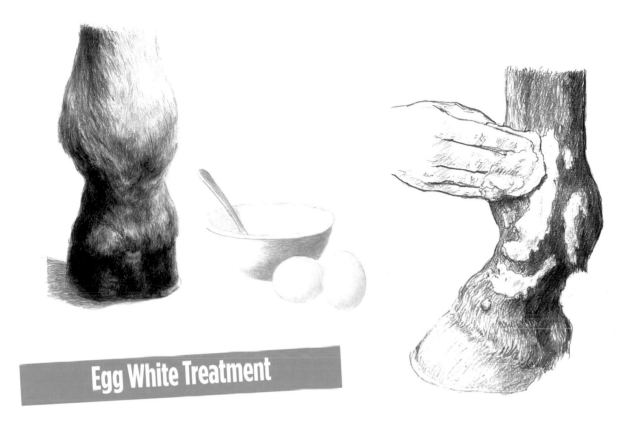

Egg White Treatment

Horses often get swollen fetlocks if they are worked too hard or bang into something. To treat the swelling, beat one or two egg whites and dab on the affected area. Massage into the skin, but be careful not to rub too hard. Cover up with gauze and a stable bandage. Repeat every day for a week, making sure that you clean the fetlock before each application. The astringent properties of the egg whites help reduce the swelling.

TAKING A HORSE'S PULSE

When you think your horse might be ailing, it's a good idea to take his pulse before calling the veterinarian. You can check your horse's pulse by pressing your fingers on any major blood vessel, but the easiest place to count his heartbeat is the mandibular artery located just under the jaw. A horse's resting heart rate is about 40 beats per minute. If his heart rate is higher, that means he has a fever. The higher the heart rate, the higher the fever.

NO MORE SKIN IRRITATION

My mare just loves watching what goes on in the stable from her stall. She's a real security guard! To encourage this behavior that keeps her entertained, I installed a chain at the entrance of her stall. This allows the door to stay open and gives her a better view of the action. Unfortunately, she leans so hard against the chain that she rubs the hair off her shoulders and breast, which causes skin irritations.

To prevent this, I covered the chain with an old garden hose. I cut the hose to the same length as the chain and threaded the chain through the hose. My mare can now push against the chain all she wants. With the hose as a buffer, she won't damage her coat!

Powder to the Rescue

Shin boots are very useful for protecting your horse's limbs. However, they can cause inflammation in the tendons, especially if the horse wears them during a crosscountry event or a long ride.

To avoid this problem, sprinkle the shin boots with talcum powder. Start by cleaning them thoroughly with a brush or sponge. Once the shin boots are dry, dust the inside with talcum powder and use your hand to spread the powder around evenly. Don't forget to make sure that your horse's limbs are also clean.

Taking Medication

I have a plain and simple trick to get horses to take powdered medication without wasting an ounce. I mix the medicine with applesauce and sometimes add in their regular pellets or flaked feed. It tastes so good that the horses lick the whole thing up, even the sides of the bucket. I have peace of mind knowing that they have received their full dose of medicine.

 # How to Recognize Good Hay

In the winter months, my horses' diet includes more hay so it's important to know how to check that it is of good quality. Most riders know that hay should have a pleasant smell and a nice green color. Here's a simple trick to test the moisture level: take a few tufts of hay in both hands and twist vigorously. The hay should be supple enough to take 10 twists, which means it is not too dry. However, if it doesn't break apart after 15 twists, that means it is too moist.

Getting Rid of Parasites

I discovered little yellow spots on my horse's limbs, which turned out to be fly eggs. These parasites are dangerous because if a horse swallows them while grooming himself, they can cause damage to his body. To get rid of them, I rub the affected areas with a sponge soaked in warm vinegar. Repeat for 2 days in a row to make sure the eggs fall off on their own.

WATER YOUR HORSE IN WINTER

I remember a time when horses were used on the farm. In winter, when horses came into the barn soaked in sweat after their day's work, we prepared a slurry to rehydrate them. Here's the recipe. We added a pot full of hot water and the same quantity of ground up barley or oats to a bucket of cold, hand-pumped water. The horses enjoyed their peck of oats while drinking enough to be fresh and ready for the next day's work.

Anchor Your Buckets

In winter, I give my horses pellets to replace the grass they would normally eat in pasture. I put their feed buckets on the ground beside the horse shelter that also doubles as my tack room. The horses have the annoying habit of overturning their buckets in their rush to eat the pellets. So I found this simple but effective solution: I run a length of baler twine through the handle of each bucket and use it to attach the buckets to the posts of the tack room. Since the buckets stay wedged against the wall, my horses can eat without spilling and wasting their pellets.

A SPOONFUL OF SUGAR

My horse can detect the least little bit of powdered medication mixed in with his pellets or hidden inside a carrot or piece of bread. He spits it right back out! Since he has a sweet tooth, I mix his medication in a spoonful of honey which I roll in some bran before adding it to his ration of pellets. Giving my horse his medication is no longer the chore it used to be!

Whistle After Work

After a workout, my horse was often so tight that he was unable to urinate. Since it was essential that he regularly eliminate his toxins, I found a simple trick to help get him to pee: after putting him in his stall, I wait for him to relax and start nibbling his straw and then I whistle. The whistling gets his attention and he relaxes the rest of this body enough to urinate. To reinforce this behavior, I started whistling each time I noticed him urinating. This way, as soon as I whistle, he associates the sound with the action of emptying his bladder. I can even make him relieve himself on command, even when he's competing in the show ring.

♫ WHISTLE AFTER, YOU WORK, WHISTLE AFTER WORK♪

WHEN THERE'S A SONG TO HELP YOU SET THE PACE ♪

IT WONT TAKE LONG♫

WHEN THEY WHISTLE, I EMPTY MY BLADDER

Measure Me!

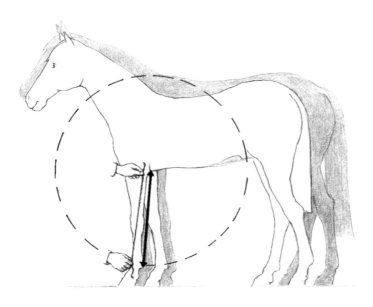

As the proud owner of a 2-year-old colt, I'm curious to know how big he'll get when he reaches adulthood. A breeder friend told me about the "string method." Measure the length of the foreleg between the back of the fetlock and the point of elbow with a piece of string. Swing the string upwards using the point of elbow as the pivot point. The other end of the string should indicate the height of the adult horse's withers.

HAIR CARE

I'm the owner of Friesian horses and spend a lot of time keeping their beautiful manes strong, silky and dandruff-free. A few years ago I found just the trick. Twice a week, I rub the root of their mane with Pétrole Hahn Lotion Vert. It works like a charm! My friends have told me that this product also works on other horse breeds.

STIMULATING HAIR GROWTH

In spite of good nutrition, regular grooming and careful untangling, my mare's tail has never been long and thick. During a routine visit to the veterinarian for vaccines, he gave me this advice to spruce up her tail. Add a can of pure malt alcohol-free beer to her daily ration. After 3 months, I noticed an improvement in the growth of her tail hairs. This spring, she'll be the belle of the pasture! This treatment is also good for stimulating hoof horn growth.

Sweet Syringe

My mare always categorically refused to take her dose of wormer and panicked as soon as she saw me coming with a syringe. Since she has a sweet tooth, I tried this technique to trick her. As a first step, which I repeated for several days, I approached her with a syringe filled with applesauce or apple juice and squeezed some out. After sniffing it, my mare was intrigued enough to try licking it. She quickly took a liking to the taste and even tried to eat the syringe! She eventually let me gently inject the applesauce directly into her mouth. This syringe has now become her favorite treat and it's easy to fill it with real wormer, disguised with the taste of apple.

BURS, BE GONE!

To remove burs from the tangled hairs in my horse's tail, I spray on a conditioner and let it sit for 5 minutes. The burs are then easier to comb out. You can also leave your horse for a couple of days in his stall or a paddock where there are no thistles. The burs will eventually dry out and fall off on their own.

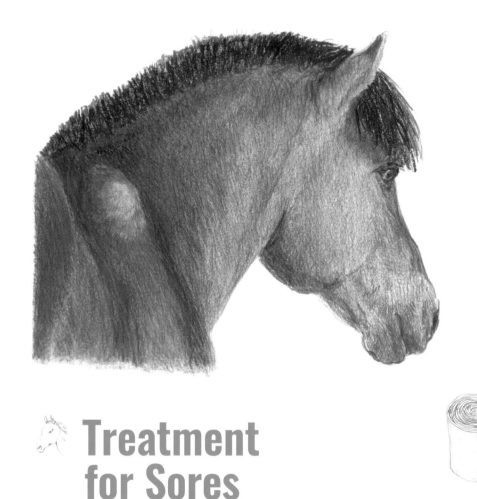

Treatment for Sores

In my riding club, horses sometimes develop saddle and girth sores. When a horse is saddled for too long or a piece of tack doesn't fit right, the rubbing causes swelling and hair loss, often in the area of the withers or the girth.

To ease the discomfort, place ice cubes in a small cloth bag or clean sock and hold it in place with a stable bandage wrapped around the horse's barrel for a few minutes to help reduce the swelling. However, this treatment shouldn't replace a good equipment check before riding your horse!

Woah, Boy!

To prevent my horse from eating too quickly, which can cause him to choke or have stomach pain, I break some pieces off a salt block and add them to his feeding trough. The salt forces him to rummage for his feed, so he's more patient and eats more slowly.

TEA TO PREVENT SCRATCHING

When my horse sheds, he scratches himself a lot. Since tea is known for its calming properties, I spray some on his coat where he's itchy. Here's my recipe. Take three or four tea bags and let them steep in boiled water. Allow the tea to cool and transfer it to a spray bottle. Spray the areas where your horse scratches himself and repeat for several days. Since I've started doing this, my horse is scratching much less than before.

A Sure Fix

My horse injured himself just above his hoof after a fall. Even though I treated it with disinfectants, healing creams and other sprays, the wound still hadn't healed 7 months later! It had even started budding.

So I mentioned it to a groom who had 35 years of experience taking care of racehorses. He suggested that I dab some Veredus Villate solution on the wound every day with a cotton swab. In 2 months, the injury had diminished and a month later, it finally healed. I also rubbed some sweet almond oil on the area after it healed to soften the skin.

TACK

TO EACH HIS OWN HALTER

Children at the pony riding club often have difficulty knowing which halter goes on which pony. As a result, they often use halters that are either too big or too small. So we decided to customize the halters by writing the pony's names on the nosebands using 3D fabric paint (available in jars or easy-to-use tubes from craft stores or stationary stores). It's waterproof and very pretty to boot!

Comfort Stirrup

Endurance riders often use "closed" stirrups with a larger tread than classic stirrups. The issue is that these types of stirrups are expensive. I found a lowcost solution: I used a cycling toe clip. I screwed the bottom part of the toe clip to the base of the stirrup and the top part of the toe clip to the sides of the stirrup and reinforced my invention with electrical tape. You can even ride in your sneakers without getting your foot stuck!

WHITEN YOUR WHITES

The best advice for cleaning white leather is not to let it get too dirty in the first place! I have one bridle that I want to keep spotless, so I clean it regularly. After removing most of the dust with a rag, I clean the white parts with a piece of cotton cloth dipped in baby cleansing milk. It's not an obvious solution, but it works and the leather remains soft, supple and clean.

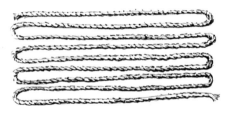

🐴 Flyswatter

All you need to make an effective, lowcost flyswatter is a ball of yarn and some scissors. The goal is to make pom-poms to attach to the bridle's cheek piece, browband and noseband. Cut a 3 foot (1 m) piece of yarn and ball it up in folds of equal length. Cut a small piece of yarn and tie it around the center of the folded yarn. Tie a 1 inch (2 cm) piece of yarn around one end of the bunched yarn below the first knot. Finally, cut the yarn on the bottom end and tie the pom-pom to the bridle.

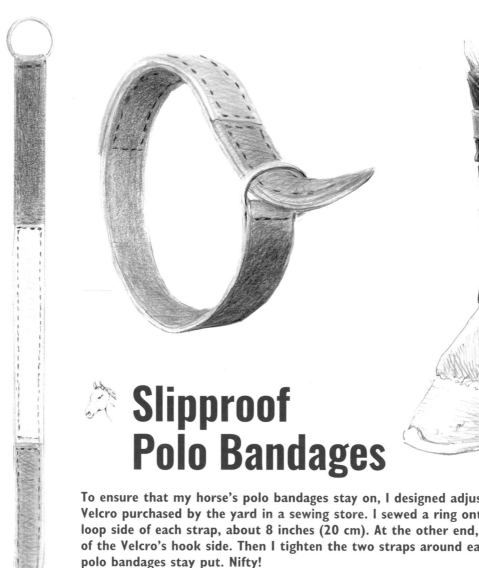

Slipproof Polo Bandages

To ensure that my horse's polo bandages stay on, I designed adjustable straps with Velcro purchased by the yard in a sewing store. I sewed a ring onto one end of the loop side of each strap, about 8 inches (20 cm). At the other end, I added a strip of the Velcro's hook side. Then I tighten the two straps around each leg and my polo bandages stay put. Nifty!

EASY ON YOUR STABLE WRAPS!

Some horses like to chew holes through the wraps that their doting owners place on their legs, and the wraps quickly become unfit for use. To deter my horses from nibbling their wraps, I slip pantyhose over them. Since the pantyhose prevents the horses from grabbing the wraps with their teeth, they quickly lose their appeal.

Safety Stirrup Rubber Ring

The rubber ring used to fasten safety stirrups can easily get snagged on branches, damaged in bad weather or burnt in the sun, so it needs to be changed regularly. However, I'm not always near a saddler's store and, to make matters worse, this item is often out of stock. Instead, I secure my safety stirrups with a rubber ring used to seal canning jars. It works fine and looks just like the real thing!

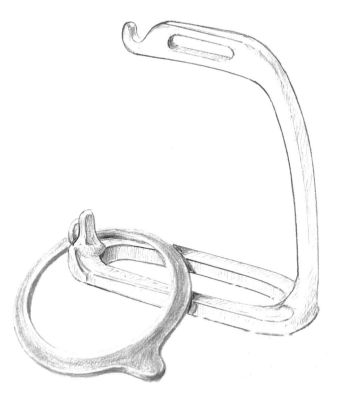

ALL TUCKED IN

My horse wears a blanket when he's in the pasture. Unfortunately, my restless friend manages to untie the straps and remove the blanket, which could cause him harm. I've developed a clever, lowcost technique to curb this undesirable behavior. I tie an elastic, like the ones used to braid horsehair, to one of the buckles on the strap and fasten it to the other buckle. If I do this to both belly straps, my horse can't undo them.

Washing Saddlecloths: What a Chore!

Washing saddlecloths isn't easy. The hair clogs up the washing machine, the stains won't come out and my beautiful white saddlecloths turn brown! I found one effective way to keep them looking new: use a high pressure washer! I add a bit of shampoo on the surface of the saddlecloth and rinse it with my washer. The stitching holds up well and the saddlecloth is restored to its original color.

A Cure for Creased Leather

The locker that I use to store my tack at the stable is quite narrow and I sometimes have to cram things in for everything to fit. As a result, my bridle often comes out creased. The creases crack the leather and eventually cause it to break. Here's a very simple trick to restore leather's suppleness: soak the creased part in a bucket of warm water for about 10 minutes and then allow to dry away from any heat source. Finish with a good coat of grease and you're done!

SOCKS FOR STIRRUP COVERS

I've never taken the time to make stirrup covers. Instead, I simply protect my stirrups with old socks that are still tight enough to hold, with a slit cut in them for the stirrup straps. And when they've done their time, they're easy to replace.

Traveling Saddle

As a freelance horseback rider, I ride many owners' horses and travel from stable to stable with my saddle. There is usually nowhere to put it down, so I designed a folding saddle rack that fastens to the back of a chair or any other horizontal bar. Start with a board about 4 inches (10 cm) wide and 24 inches (60 cm) long and attach a 20 inch (50 cm) saddle support to it using a hinge (C). To keep the saddle support horizontal, install a removable brace (D) that rests in a notch (F) at the bottom of the vertical board and against a stop (B) in the horizontal board. A small leather strap (E) can be used to fasten the saddle rack to the back of a chair and to keep the device folded when not in use. The last step is to create a small hole (A) at the top of the vertical board to thread the leather through. All done!

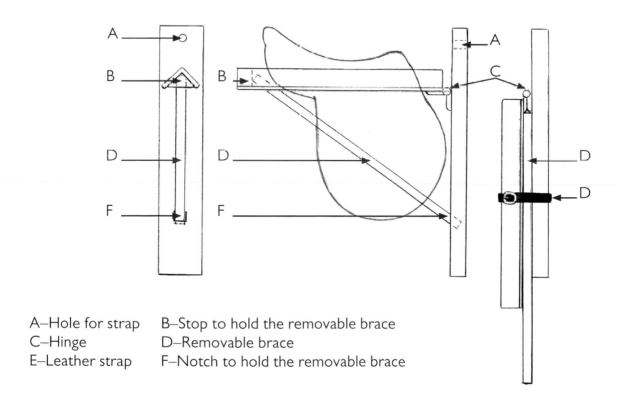

A—Hole for strap   B—Stop to hold the removable brace
C—Hinge   D—Removable brace
E—Leather strap   F—Notch to hold the removable brace

Custom Reins

My horse has a very long neck. My reins were fine for working, but they were too short to allow my horse to graze when we went horseback riding. I always ended up propped up on my horse's neck with my standard reins – not the safest! I now use a set of pony-sized draw reins. They're perfect!

SADDLE HOLDER

I found a cheap and simple way to avoid leaving my saddle on the ground or in dirty hay in the stall when I brush my horse after a ride. All you need is a lunge and a whip. Thread the whip through the snap hook at the end of the lunge and tie the lunge to a tie ring or a stall bar, leaving it about 8 inches (20 cm) longer than the saddle. Simply rest your saddle on the lunge and secure it with the whip, as shown in the image. The saddle will hold on its own! The nice thing about this solution is that it takes up very little room once you remove the saddle.

LOWCOST REINS

I could never find reins to fit my pony, so I used a mountaineering strap and added snap hooks to each end using rivets. Then I simply snapped the strap to my pony's bit. My reins were the length I wanted them to be!

Stay, Saddle!

My horse is slightly plump and sometimes the girth hurts him where it gets wedged between his belly and his elbow. All you need to keep the saddle from slipping forward are three reins and four girth sleeves. Cut a slit width-wise in two of the girth sleeves, thread a rein through each and loop each rein around each side of your horse's girth. You should have two reins with sleeves on either side of your horse. Cut the third rein to a length of 2.5 to 3 feet (80 cm to 1 m), depending on your horse's size and breed. Thread it through the third girth sleeve and cut a slit on each end. Thread the two reins on each side of your horse through the slits and tie them at the rear of your mount, remembering to put the fourth girth sleeve in place to prevent chafing. Leave everything loose enough to keep your horse comfortable.

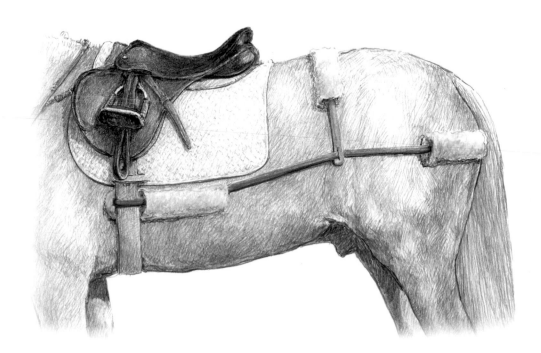

Keep That Blanket On!

My horse is a bit too small for his blanket. As a result, the girths have a tendency to come undone during the night. How many times have I had to throw out his blanket after finding it torn to shreds? Plus, a loose blanket could snag on just about anything and cause an accident. To keep the clasps from coming undone, I use small rubber gaskets found on swing-top glass bottles and wrap them around the "T" in the clasps. The clasps are securely wedged and do not come undone, so my horse stays covered all night.

A BAG TO STORE GROOMING EQUIPMENT

I wanted a practical, sturdy, lowcost one-of-a-kind bag with many pockets to store all my grooming equipment, so I decided to make one. I took an old pair of small jeans, cut off the legs and sewed the four layers of fabric together with a sturdy seam. I added a strap, and my work was done! I now have four pockets to store my hoof pick, my comb, my horsehair elastics … and a fun and nifty bag that didn't cost a cent!

FROM SPUR TO HALTER HOOK

I'm always looking for crafty and handy ways to store my tack and decorate my tack room. I found a way to reuse my old spurs. Once they are nice and clean, I hammered a large staple to secure one of the arms of the spurs onto a wooden board. The other arm can be used as a hook to hang halters and bridles.

Handmade Net

You can make your own haynet using baler twine. All you need are 14 strands of twine, without knots, each measuring about 6 feet (2 m). Make a loop with one of the strands by tying both ends together (1) and twist it three times in a figure eight to form a single loop measuring about 4 inches (10 cm) in diameter (2). Tie 12 strands at equal distances around this loop using slip knots (3). Once they are all fastened, tie each strand to the one next to it about 4 inches (10 cm) down from the top (4). For best results, aim for equal distances. Repeat this step until the eighth or tenth row, depending on the desired size. To finish the net, cut the strands about 1 inch (2 cm) from the last row of knots. Weave the remaining strand of twine through the mesh of the last row (5). Once this last strand is tied with a knot, you can use it to open and close the net and to hang it. As a finishing touch, you can also slip small rings into the knots on the bottom row and thread the last strand of twine through the rings. Remember to hang your haynet high enough so your horse can't get his legs caught in the mesh when the net is empty.

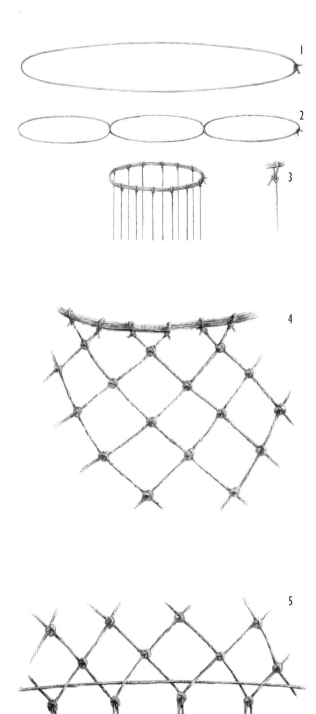

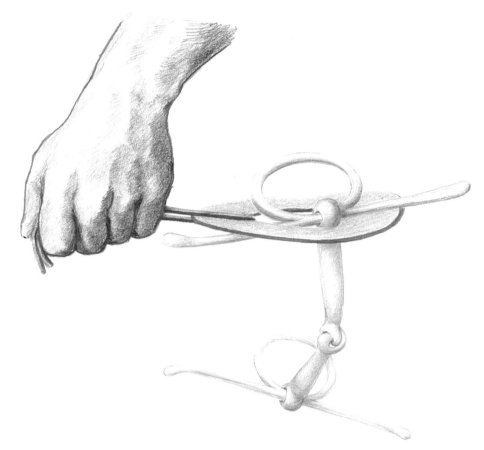

Malleable Bit Guards

Attaching brand new rubber bit guards to a full cheek snaffle can be tricky since they are not easy to stretch. To soften them up, I place them in a pot of boiling water for just under a minute. I can then easily pull the bit guard over the side of the bit using a shoelace or a leather strap.

SPOTLESS STIRRUPS

When it rains, stirrups get covered in mud or sand, which can get your saddle dirty and cause wear and tear. I came up with a trick to avoid having to clean them after each use.

I made small covers for my stirrups. I cut the bottom of the legs off an old pair of jeans. The width of the leg should be about the same as that of the stirrup. I cut it a few inches longer than needed and folded the seam down to sew a casing for a shoelace. I then stitched the bottom of the cover, leaving an opening for the stirrup leather. It's a simple, quick and lowcost way to keep my saddle looking good even in bad weather.

Stirrup Covers

Winter weather can really wreak havoc on stirrups. When I pull them up, they often end up damaging the saddle or getting it dirty where they knock or rub against the saddle flaps. So I decided to make two small covers out of terry cloth (slightly wider than a washcloth) that I slip onto the stirrups to protect my saddle when the stirrups are pulled up. I added an elastic at the top of each cover to tighten the opening and left a large slit on each side for the stirrup leathers. It's a simple yet effective way to protect your saddle!

TWO NOSEBANDS IN ONE

When wearing his cavesson noseband, my horse would open his mouth and slip his tongue on top of the bit. A flash noseband would have been more suitable. To avoid purchasing a new noseband, I bought a small leather strap and placed it around the cavesson noseband, thereby preventing my horse from being able to move his tongue to avoid the bit.

LITTER BUG!

 # Blanket Storage

Before the cold weather hits, I dig out my blankets and exercise rugs that I store in my garage. I am often unpleasantly surprised to find them chewed to pieces by mice. What a mess! I came up with an easy way to keep these critters at bay. After cleaning the blankets, I store them in a large garbage bag filled with dried mint sprigs. My blankets stay intact and smell nice and fresh!

PAINTED PITCHFORK

We sometimes forget our pitchfork in the stable or stall, which can be a hazard for the horses. So I came up with a simple trick to spot a pitchfork in a glance: paint the bottom white. This way, it's easy to see and I'm less likely to forget it in the stable.

FEED BAG HAMMOCK

We like to go riding and we bring our horses with us everywhere. In the horse trailer, the hay tends to fall out of the net and onto the ground, out of the horses' reach. So I made them a large fabric feed bag. I tie one side of it to the partition grid and the other side to the breast bar with cotton cords. The hay falls into the raised feed bag "hammock" instead of onto the ground, making it easy for the horses to reach it. We leave the feed bag there for the duration of the trip. The bag sways with the trailer and there is always hay available to the horses. When we stop and need to reach the horses, we just unhook it from the chest bar. Very handy!

Sheepskin Saddle Pads

To extend the life of my sheepskin saddle pad, I soak it for a few minutes in a large basin of lukewarm water and then wash it with my own volumizing shampoo. I scrub it with a nail brush to avoid damaging the pad. This process puffs the pad back up. Remember to rinse and wring (by hand) to avoid damp smells. Most importantly, avoid direct heat sources (such as electric baseboard heaters), as heat exposure may shrivel this type of equipment.

LIKE NEW

I have a copper bit that turned green with verdigris over time. Luckily, my grandmother shared her secret for cleaning copper pots and it worked with my bit. Squeeze the juice of half a lemon over the bit and scrub vigorously with coarse salt. Wear gloves when you do this, as the salt is very abrasive. Rinse the bit with clean water and you're done!

DIY Rope Halter

With a little patience, you can make your own halter following these simple steps! Examine all the illustrations before you begin to understand and visualize the steps.

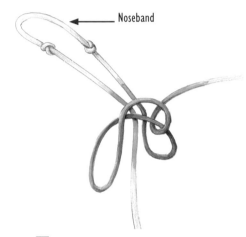

Noseband

8 feet (2.5m)

11 feet (3.5m)

10 inches (25 cm)

1 You'll need a quarter-inch (6 mm) diameter rope measuring 20 feet (6 m). Work on a table to make the knots on a flat surface. Make a square knot about 8 feet (2.5 m) (green) and another about 11 feet (3.5 m) (pink) from the end of the rope. This is the start of the noseband.

2 This is the foundation of the most complex knot, the one that will create the loop that will allow you to attach the lunge to the base of the noseband.

3 Make this knot carefully by pulling the four ends of the rope simultaneously, but without tightening too quickly. The challenge is to adjust both of the noseband's cheekpieces so that they are even (about 8 inches or 20 cm). You'll have to play with the rope a bit to balance out the length of each cheekpiece.

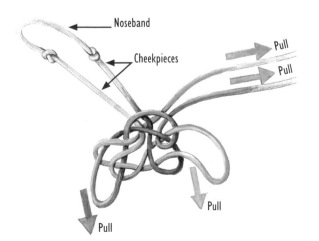

Noseband

Cheekpieces

Pull
Pull
Pull
Pull

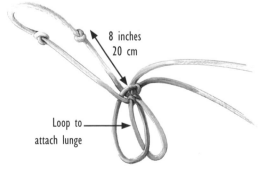

8 inches 20 cm

Loop to attach lunge

4 Once each cheekpiece is the right length, tighten the knot to create the loop that will be used to attach the lunge.

98

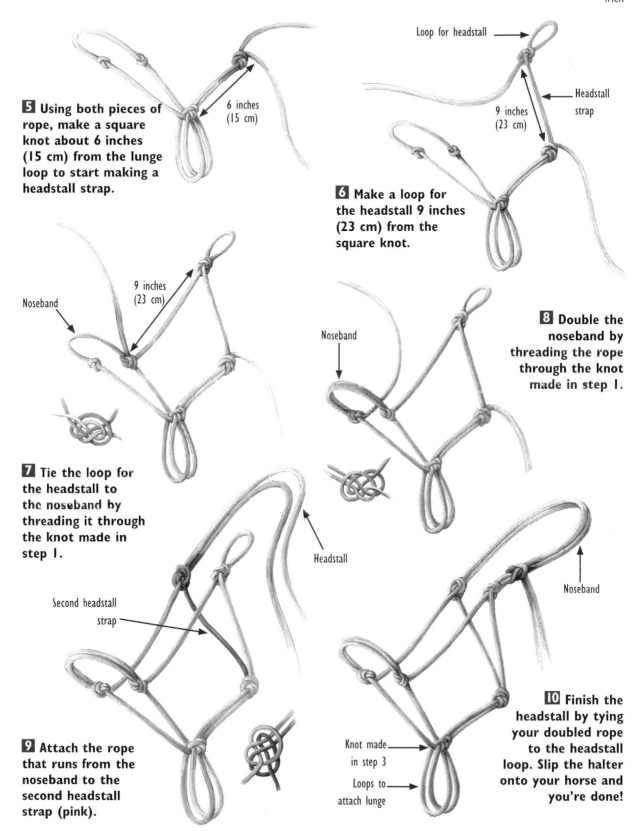

5 Using both pieces of rope, make a square knot about 6 inches (15 cm) from the lunge loop to start making a headstall strap.

6 inches (15 cm)

Loop for headstall

Headstall strap

9 inches (23 cm)

6 Make a loop for the headstall 9 inches (23 cm) from the square knot.

Noseband

9 inches (23 cm)

Noseband

8 Double the noseband by threading the rope through the knot made in step 1.

7 Tie the loop for the headstall to the noseband by threading it through the knot made in step 1.

Second headstall strap

Headstall

Noseband

9 Attach the rope that runs from the noseband to the second headstall strap (pink).

Knot made in step 3

Loops to attach lunge

10 Finish the headstall by tying your doubled rope to the headstall loop. Slip the halter onto your horse and you're done!

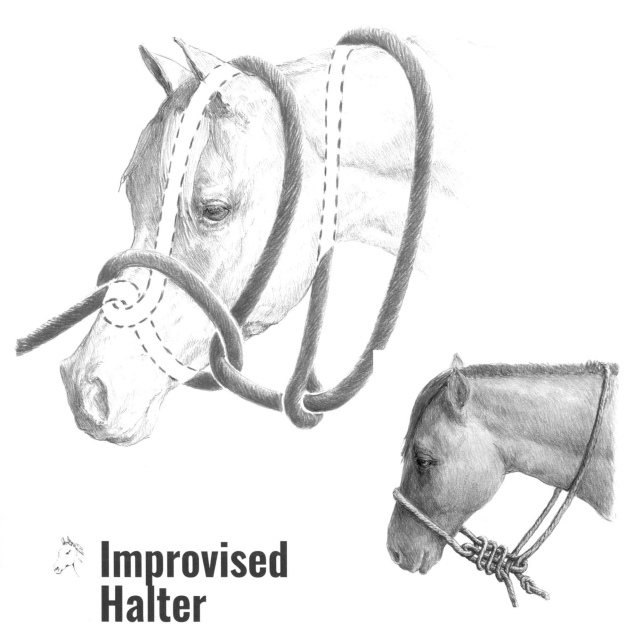

Improvised Halter

I often forget my halter when I venture out to the paddock to bring my horse back to the stable. I've therefore had to make do with the rope that I leave near the pasture fence to secure the gate. I found a way to use this rope as an improvised halter, a better solution than simply placing it around the horse's neck. I either use simple loops or a modified noose. Refer to the illustrations to choose your preferred method.

REMOVING RUST
FROM A BIT OR HALTER

When I came across a rusted western bit, I obviously didn't want my horse to use it in that condition. So I used a tried and true method to clean it: I simply soaked the mouthpiece in cola for a few hours. The older the rust, the longer the bit will need to soak (I let mine soak overnight). You may even need to repeat the process several times. I used a scrubbing sponge at the end and was very happy with the results!

Lunges Made With Twine

When your horses like to chew on rope, you need to either constantly buy new lunges or find a more cost-efficient solution! I make my own leads with twine used for round bales of hay (usually blue) or square bales of hay (orange). Just follow these simple steps: Cut several strands of twine (depending on how thick you want your lead) of equal length, but do not make a knot. Ask a helper to hold one end of the strands while you hold the other end. Keeping a good grip, both of you need to turn your strands in the same direction (both clockwise, for instance). Keep the rope taut to prevent the strands from twisting. Once you have finished turning the rope and the strands are nice and taut, a third person stands at the center of the rope and folds it in half (the people on each end come together while holding the rope taut, ensuring that it does not twist in every direction). The third person guides the rope so that the two strands twist around each other evenly from the middle. To finish, tie a knot and burn the ends with a lighter to prevent the strands from coming apart.

Clean as New

We've all had to deal with bits that are hard to clean with just water. If it's not washed after each use, the steel becomes stained and coated with leftover pellets or hay. I found a solution! I scrub the bit with baking soda using a sponge dipped in lukewarm water. Then I soak the bit for half an hour and rinse it thoroughly with clean water. This method leaves the bit tasteless and safe for our horses!

Comfort Stirrup

Endurance riders often use "closed" stirrups with a larger tread than classic stirrups. The issue is that these types of stirrups are expensive. I found a low-cost solution: I used a cycling toe clip. I screwed the bottom part of the toe clip to the base of the stirrup and the top part of the toe clip to the sides of the stirrup and reinforced my invention with electrical tape. You can even ride in your sneakers without getting your foot stuck!

WHITEN YOUR WHITES

The best advice for cleaning white leather is not to let it get too dirty in the first place! I have one bridle that I want to keep spotless, so I clean it regularly. After removing most of the dust with a rag, I clean the white parts with a piece of cotton cloth dipped in baby cleansing milk. It's not an obvious solution, but it works and the leather remains soft, supple and clean.

Spruced Up Protective Gear

I like to customize my things, like changing the color of my horse's rubber bell boots. To do this, buy some aerosol paint from a craft store and follow these simple steps. Cover your work surface with a piece of cardboard. Place a bell boot on the cardboard and spray it with the aerosol paint. Let it dry for 24 hours before applying a second coat, if needed. You might still see some marks if you look closely but they'll be indistinguishable from far away. Tip: use the aerosol paint outdoors and wear a mask to avoid inhaling toxic fumes. You can also make a design on the boot (here, a flower) using a piece of cardboard temporarily applied to the boot and removed after the paint is sprayed.

MANURE REMOVAL

It's impossible to remove a bag of manure from a regular garbage can without breaking the bag. To solve this, I cut the bottom out of a cylindrical drum and attached two handles to it. To remove the plastic garbage bag full of manure, simply lift the cylinder. The smooth interior of the cylinder prevents the bag from tearing.

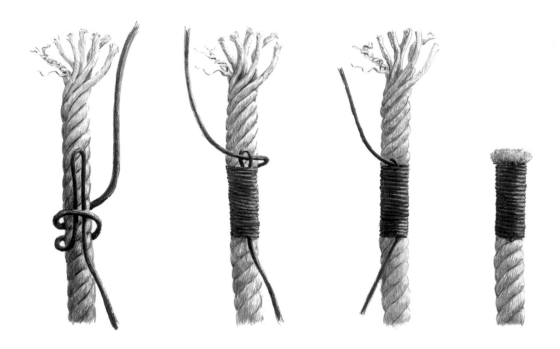

KEEP DUST IN CHECK

A simple sweep of the broom can create a cloud of dust, especially in a stable. This often triggered my allergies. To avoid this, I use a garden sprinkler to create a fine mist before sweeping. The moisture keeps the dust under control. I can then sweep without worrying about inhaling dust particles.

 # Wear-Resistant Lunges

Rope lunges deteriorate with use and start to unravel after getting stepped on by horses or damaged by rain. I tried holding them together with thick, ultra-strong tape but it always ended up peeling off. My solution: I surround the frayed end of the lunge with a smaller cord with the end folded to make a loop pointed toward the damaged end of the lunge. I then tightly wrap the long end of the cord around the lunge and the loop and finish with a knot by threading the cord inside the loop. Finally, I cut the excess strands of the lunge and burn them with a flame. The tip is neat and I can continue using my lunge.

Makeshift Martingale

My Shetland has the annoying habit of lifting his head to avoid being controlled, but every standing martingale we tried was too big for him.

My instructor found another solution. We hook one end of a horse-sized stirrup leather to Cachou's very loose noseband and the other end to his girth. Make sure that the stirrup leather passes right between the horse's legs. You can add a layer of sheepskin to prevent chafing.

Secure Halter

It's harder for a horse to remove his own halter if it's held in place with a braid. Simply take one strand in front of the headstall and two strands behind it, and you have an attractive way to deter your horse from removing his halter.

BRUSH HOLDER

I'm always searching for my brushes. Since they're usually lying in the hay near the stalls, I can never find them and often step on them. So I made a little holder for them. I stood a log measuring approximately 3 inches (7 cm) in diameter and 20 inches (50 cm) long on a wooden board about 12 inches (30 cm) square and 1 inch (2 cm) thick. I nailed the log into the board and hammered a few small nails into the log. Now, I have a brush holder. Just add a little handle to the brushes that don't have any and you're done!

Versatile Tires

In the stable or in the pasture, my horse is constantly playing with his trough and spilling its contents. So I set the trough inside an old tire to prevent my horse from tipping it over. But once he was finished eating, my mischievous friend would remove the trough from the tire and play with it only to abandon it in the field. With its sides all chewed up, the trough quickly became unfit for use. So I drilled two holes on either side of his trough and secured it to the tire with bolts and washers. Now it stays put! An old tire can also be very useful in the stable: wrap half a tire around the edge of a pail to prevent injuries. It can also be used as a slalom block or a jump standard.

KEEPING THE MASK ON

In the summer, I put a fly mask on my horse to protect him from mosquitoes. However, he discovered how to lean up against a pole in the pasture to remove the mask by pulling on the thick Velcro elastic under his lower jaw. Consequently, every day I would find his mask trampled in the field. I solved this problem by shortening the elastic until the two sides of the mask touched. All you need is thread, a needle, three small stitches and your problem is solved. My horse now keeps his mask on and is safe from mosquitoes.

Another simple and efficient solution: I place a rope halter over top of the mask. This way, my mare can't remove it.

Removable Feeding Trough

I prefer using a removable feeding trough (a pail holder with hooks) that I hang on the door of my mare's stall because it's easier to clean. The only problem was that my rascal of a horse would regularly knock it down. So I sawed two notches in the stall door for the hooks. Then I installed two latches on the outside of the door to hold the hooks in place. My mare can no longer move her trough but I can still remove it for cleaning simply by unlatching it! She hasn't figured out how to unlatch it herself ... yet!

MY HORSE REMOVES HIS BRIDLE

I have a trick for horses who like to remove their bridles by brushing up against trees while riding. We keep the halter under the bridle when we go out. Since the halter is harder to remove, I tie the two headstalls together with Velcro ties. This trick keeps the bridle from slipping in front of the ears.

Cleaning Leather

When your leather bridle has tar stains on it, buy some montmorillonite from your drugstore and sprinkle a small amount on the stains. Montmorillonite is absorbent and will work well on fresh stains. The older the stain, the longer you need to leave this natural clay-based product on the leather. Let it sit and wipe with a rag.

Another solution: scrape the tar off with a spoon and coat the stain with talcum powder mixed with benzene, a solvent also found in drugstores. Some people simply rub butter on the stain with a rag. A small amount of talcum powder will remove the butter's greasy residue.

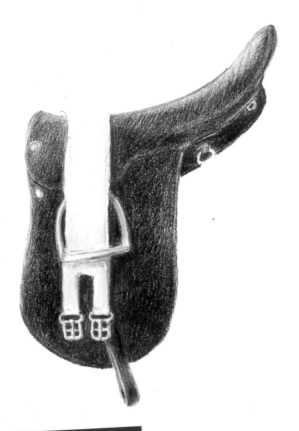

Carrying Your Saddle

After unsaddling my horse, carrying the saddle along with the bridle, saddlecloth and saddle pad is always quite cumbersome. With the bridle draped over my shoulder, the saddle under my arm, the cantle on my hip and the saddlecloth and saddle pad piled on top, it's tricky to keep everything balanced! When the girth slips off and the stirrups swing down and hit me in the knees, I reach my breaking point. So I found a better way to organize things: after lifting the stirrups up, I thread the girth through the stirrup, fold the girth on top of the saddle and slide it through the second stirrup. Everything holds together better and I can make it to the tack room without losing any equipment on the way. No more frustration!

PORTABLE MOUNTING BLOCK

My horse is so tall that mounting him feels like mountain climbing! Hoisting yourself onto your horse by pulling on his saddle isn't good for the horse's back, either. So I bought a folding stool (available in a saddler's store or hardware store). It's the perfect mounting block. Since it folds, I can put it in my truck when I go to competitions (it's very compact) and it's easy to carry. I take it everywhere!

QUICK CLEAN-UP

Most riders clean their leather saddles with glycerin saddle soap and grease. But what about synthetic saddles? I've been told to clean mine with a sponge and water, but that takes hours to dry. I found a much more practical solution that requires no drying time: baby wipes! Plus, you don't have to dip your hands in cold water to get the sponge wet in winter!

110

Stable Bridle Holder

The stalls at the riding center where I board my mare are far from the tack room. To avoid making several trips, I bring my saddle and my bridle together. But there's no hook near the stall for my bridle. So I made a removable bridle holder out of a steel plate. Using a vise and a hammer, I shaped a 0.1 inch (3 mm) thick flat steel plate into a hook that I can install on the top edge of the stall door to hang my equipment. You can also use rebar, which is thinner and easier to shape, but just as sturdy.

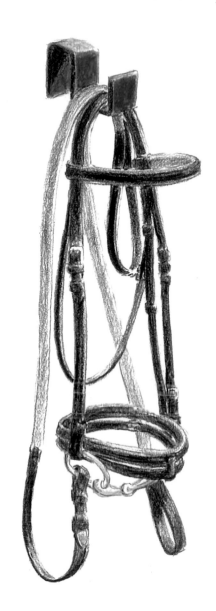

HOW TO CLEAN VELCRO

In the summer, I put a fly mask with Velcro straps on my horse. The Velcro straps are very handy … except when it comes time to clean them. Since scrubbing them with a dandy brush or tossing them in the washing machine doesn't work, I suggest using a file cleaner available at any hardware store.

Another solution: small metal brushes sold in pet stores.

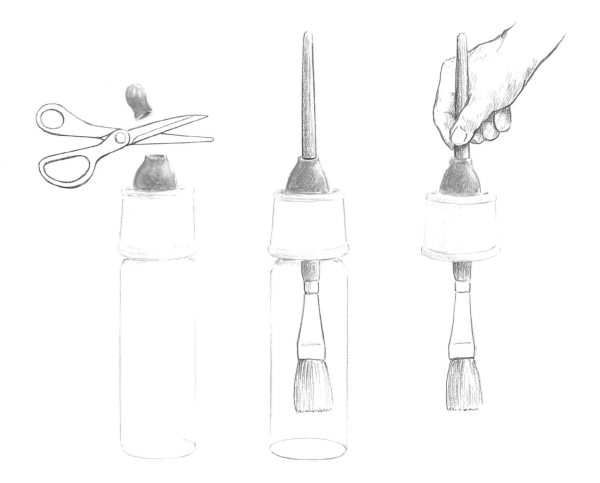

Brush Storage

I was looking for a way to neatly store the brush I use to grease my horse's feet. The handle was always full of grease, which made my hands greasy too, and the bristles got damaged because the brush was just left loose in my grooming box. So I bought a regular baby nursing bottle in a department store. I cut off the top half of the nipple and slid the brush handle into the hole to keep the bristles inside the bottle. With the handle on the outside, I just unscrew the top of the bottle when I want to grease my horse's hooves. Not only do my hands stay clean, but the bristles stay intact and the rest of my tack is protected from the grease.

Brush Holder

When I'm greasing my horse's feet, I often find my brush sitting in the jar where I left it, covered in grease. Sometimes I simply can't find it because I can't remember where I put it. So I had the simple idea of screwing an L-screw halfway into the brush's wooden handle. Now I can just hang the brush on the edge of the jar. The brush stays clean and I always know where to find it!

HANDY BRUSH

To keep my grease brush from smearing everything in my grooming box, I made a brush cap using materials I already had on hand. All you need is a paintbrush with a hole in the handle (or make the hole yourself), a cap from a can of shaving cream and two elastics (one regular size and one large). First, make two holes in the plastic cap using the hot tip of a center punch. Slide the smaller elastic through the holes and knot the ends. Use the larger elastic to tie the brush to the smaller elastic. This makeshift cap won't be in your way when you want to use your brush!

KNOW WHEN TO FOLD THEM!

When I wash my stable wraps or polo bandages, they have the annoying tendency to get all twisted and tangled and it's frustrating to have to separate them each time. To avoid this, I simply fold them twice lengthwise and secure them with a safety pin to ensure they don't come undone during the wash. No more wasting time untangling knots!

Storing Wraps

When I travel to competitions, I store all my tack in a trunk, including my polo bandages and stable wraps, which inevitably unravel during the trip. It's so annoying to open the grooming trunk only to find the wraps you had carefully packed completely unraveled and covered in dust.

To prevent unraveling, I tuck the edge of the rolled wrap into the second or third layer. For storage, I use a 0.5 gallon (2 l) plastic bottle cut in half. I cut a large enough slot along the neck side of the bottle to be able to easily slide the rolled wrap inside. Problem solved!

I found a lowcost way to store my stable wraps or polo bandages. I made a pair of shorts by cutting the legs off an old pair of jeans and cut the legs in half again. Using heavy-duty thread, I stitched the two parts with the thickest seams together to make the bottom of the bag. I then sewed the other two sides together and finished the top of the bag on the sewing machine. The final step is to add a drawstring to close the bag. You can also decorate your bag with heat transfer designs to add a personal touch and make it really unique.

HOMEMADE GREASE POT

My horse doesn't watch where he steps when he's tied up. Just my luck, this time he stepped on a brand new pot of hoof grease and smashed the plastic to smithereens.

In order to store the grease and keep it fit for use even in the summer, I placed a bag in a plastic flower pot that I picked up at a garden center. The flower pot needs to be slightly larger than the original pot of grease. I discarded the broken pieces of plastic from the pot of grease and set it inside its new watertight container. Good as new!

Twine Brush

I had long been looking for an easy way to clean my buckets and other containers, and I came up with a solution. I designed my own synthetic "twine brush." It's an easy, lowcost and eco-friendly way to reuse spare pieces of baler twine. Making a brush is easy: grab several strands of twine, fold them together and knot them a few times to create a compact brush that's easy to grip. You'll be pleased with the results!

NO MORE WRINKLES!

Sometimes some of my tack, especially the stirrup leathers, gets wrinkled because of moisture or improper use. Once it's been creased, leather can crack or tear if it's left in that state. To avoid this, soak the item in lukewarm water for about 10 minutes without any soap or detergent and let it dry away from any heat source to stretch out the leather. Finally, apply grease with a brush and allow the leather to absorb it.

Custom Saddle Protector

After investing in a new saddle, I absolutely wanted to protect it from dust and humidity with a vinyl saddle protector. But if I pull the stirrups up underneath, the saddle protector constantly comes undone, rides up near the flaps and doesn't protect the saddle at all! Since I also use the saddle protector to ride in bad weather, I really had to find a way to attach it more firmly to the saddle. I simply unstitched the edge of the vinyl that covers the elastic where the stirrup leathers go. Then, I firmly stitched the elastic into the vinyl on both ends. My saddle protector no longer slides off and the stirrups can still move freely.

PAINTED PITCHFORK

We sometimes forget our pitchfork in the stable or stall, which can be a hazard for the horses. So I came up with a simple trick to spot a pitchfork in a glance: paint the bottom white. This way, it's easy to see and I'm less likely to forget it in the stable.

Reinforced Feeding Trough

My uncle's horses have the habit of breaking their feeding troughs, so to avoid buying new ones each month he reinforced them with old horseshoes. He soldered horseshoes all around the plastic container using a wet sponge, one right side up, one right side down, leaving a space at the back of the trough. He centered two horseshoes to protect the bottom of the bucket and used two more to make a handle to hang the trough on the top board of the gate. He used five more horseshoes as a support under the lower board for stability. A simple yet ironclad solution!

Fixing a Broken Stirrup Leather with String

My stirrup leather unexpectedly snapped while I was out riding! I used a piece of string to fix it so I could continue riding comfortably. I joined both stirrup leathers so that the holes lined up, wrapped the string around them and threaded both ends of the string together through the top hole and back through the next hole. Then I brought both ends of the string to the front and made a double knot to hold the stirrup leather in place.

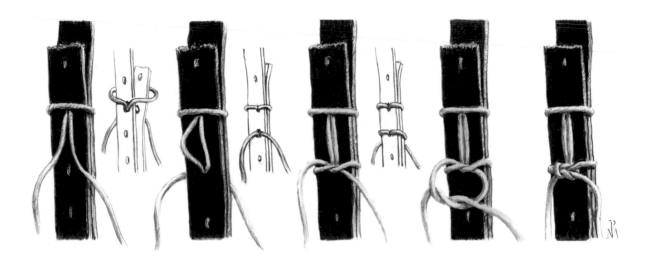

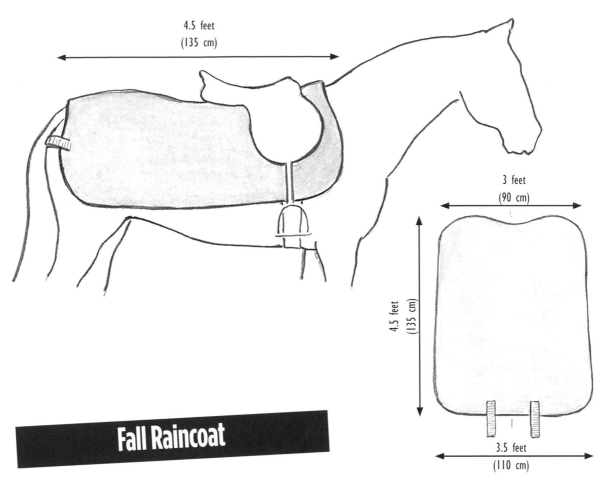

Fall Raincoat

With the rainy fall weather upon us, I wanted to keep my horse dry with a waterproof exercise rug, but these are usually quite expensive. So I made a cheaper one using an old plastic tablecloth (a waterproof tarp would also work). I cut a large rectangular tablecloth to fit the length of his back (from his withers to the base of his tail, about 4.5 feet or 135 cm), measuring 3 feet (90 cm) wide in the front and 3.5 feet (110 cm) wide in the back. For best results, topstitch the edges to prevent fraying. The exercise rug should sit between the saddlecloth and the saddle. To keep the sheet from moving, I sewed a 12 inch (30 cm) fabric band on the back with a slit in the middle and Velcro to secure it under the horse's tail. You could also make a hole where the saddle sits (make it an inch longer and wide enough to go under the flaps without getting wedged), cut the front and sew on some Velcro for easy removal.

REVAMPING AN OLD CROP

After many years of good use, the fabric around my riding crop started to fray. So I decided to use electrical tape to fix it. Electrical tape is an insulating, antistatic and nonconductive tape made of tar and latex; since it is malleable and stretchy, it can be tightened as you wrap it. Simply ensure that you apply it carefully and change it regularly.

Wrap the tape once straight around the crop about an inch (2 cm) from the damaged area. Then, keeping the tape taut, begin overlapping the previous layer (about 30 percent) as you continue to wrap the tape around the crop. Finish off with another straight wrap around the crop an inch (2 cm) above the damaged area. The repair will be seamless. Why not have a little fun and use different colors? Blue, yellow, red ... you pick!

FIXING A HALTER

I don't like throwing out tack and we always seem to need an extra halter. So I decided to revamp an old halter that had a damaged and nearly broken noseband. I used a strap from a flash noseband and tied it to the rings of the halter using a loop and a snap hook. I now have a spare halter that I'm not afraid of damaging and that I can use to go fetch the horses in any weather. I save my beautiful leather halter for competitions!

Restored Leather

While cleaning the tack room at a riding club where I worked as an intern, I found some old leather that could still be put to good use. So I used turpentine to restore it. Wearing gloves, I washed the leather with soapy water, making sure to remove any caked-on dirt. After it dried, I rubbed it with turpentine using a soft rag. It's like new! Simply maintain it using regular leather grease.

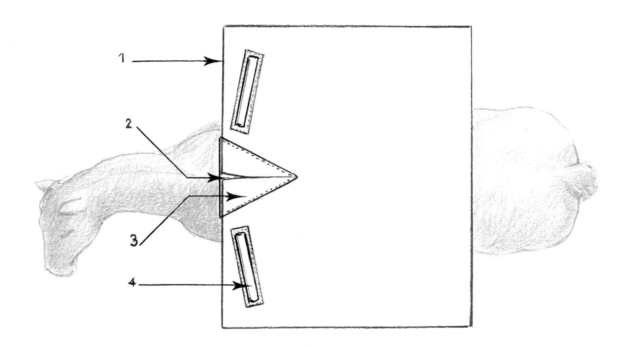

A Perfect Saddlecloth

My horse sweats profusely outdoors and his saddlecloths take forever to dry. So to keep him warm, I began sliding a thin absorbent polyester fiber vet bed between his back and the saddlecloth. To make room for his withers, I cut a slit lengthwise down the middle and added a triangular piece of fabric on each side. On the inside, I sewed two closed pockets to hold foam insulation tubes measuring 5 inches (14 cm) in diameter that prevent the saddlecloth from slipping. I never take my horse out without his vet bed!

SADDLE PACK

I always pack a lot when I go riding, and it's very cumbersome. Here's a useful tip for outdoor excursions: I use a 3 feet x 6 feet (1 m x 2 m) oilcloth as a bag. I pierce two or three small holes in it and thread laces through them to hold the pack. I spread the sheet on the ground, lay my sleeping bag and clothes on the opposite side of the holes and fold the cloth over top and on each side of my belongings. I then roll everything up and tie it with the laces. The laces have to be long enough to attach the pack to the back of the saddle. My baggage is secure, and I can reuse the tarp as a tent or a carpet.

Makeshift Saddlebags

I needed saddlebags to go riding but couldn't find any at my local saddler's store, so I made a pair. I used two small backpacks and tied them together with a fanny pack. I then placed everything in front of my saddle. I threaded the backpack straps through the girth straps to hold the bags in place. You can also set the bags behind the saddle (especially if you use larger backpacks). My horse and I are ready to ride!

WELL PACKED SADDLEBAGS

When I go riding, I hang saddlebags on my saddle. However, during the ride my things tend to shift inside the bags and get all shaken up. When I open my saddlebags when we stop for a rest, everything is a mess!

I found a solution: I save square or rectangular half-gallon (1.5 l or 2 l) plastic bottles (fruit juice bottles, for instance) and 1 gallon (5 l) water bottles. I cut the tops off and pack my items inside the bottles so they stay put. I also use the puffy aluminum bags used in 1 gallon (5 l) or 2 gallon (10 l) box wine to fill the remaining empty space in the saddlebags. These can also be used as a pillow when I stop for a nap!

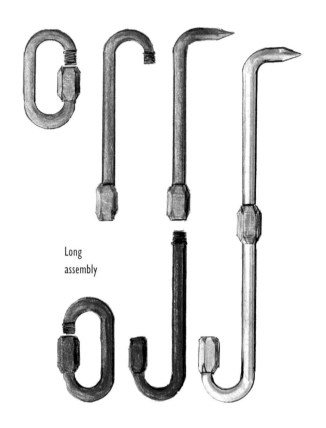

Long assembly

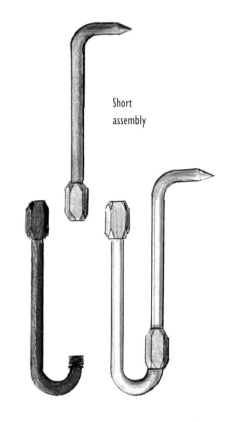

Short assembly

Pocket-Sized Hoof Pick

I often lose my hoof pick when I attend competitions, so I made a pocket-sized hoof pick that I keep with me at all times. I used chain connector links and opened them up using a vise. I shaped the first one like a cane or an umbrella handle, and straightened the second one. To make sure this would work, I tested the links to ensure they could be screwed together. I bent the end of the second link into a right angle and sharpened the tip until it was pointy. Open or closed, my hoof pick is always ready to use!

Closed

PROTECT YOUR PROTECTIVE GEAR

In horse vaulting competitions, your horse must be impeccable for the judges. But after the warm-up, your horse's leg wraps will inevitably be dirty. Lunge trainers have a very handy trick to avoid getting mud on their horse's wraps: they cover them with protective gear. You can buy this type of gear or you could use a pair or two of ski shin boots and slip them onto the horse's legs over the wraps. Just remember to take them off before the competition begins!

A Rack for Your Crop

I sometimes needed a crop when working my horse in the warmup ring. My challenge was knowing where to put it when I didn't need it so I could easily find it again. As a result, I often ended up leaving it in the sand inside the ring where I would forget it or lose it! To solve this problem, I repurposed an object that usually gets installed on the tack room wall in the stable: a lowcost whip rack available in any equestrian store. I attached it to a post in the warmup ring to give me easy access to my riding crop. I also use it to store a whip for obstacle training and a lunging whip for lungetraining.

SECOND WIND

A friend gave me one of her old rope halters, but it was worn around the noseband. So I took an old faux fur car seat cover and cut a rectangle to cover the length and width of the noseband, including the knots. I then sewed the fabric around the noseband.
I even had enough to cover the headstall!

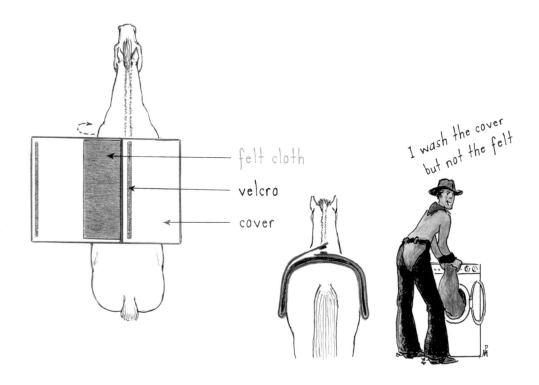

felt cloth

velcro

cover

I wash the cover but not the felt

Saddlecloth Cover

I use large saddlecloths made of felt. They're nice and thick and very comfortable for my horse, but they take forever to dry when they're soaked in sweat and they can't be machine washed. So I made a cotton cover and sewed a Velcro strip on it so it closes like a pouch. I slide my saddlecloth inside, close the pouch and throw it on my horse's back. My saddlecloth is protected and I just need to wash the cover when it gets dirty.

SECURE GIRTH, HAPPY RIDER!

When I carry my saddle, I'm always worried that the girth will slip off the seat and hit me in the shin. So I have a trick to keep it secure. When I place the girth on the seat, I thread it through the right stirrup that I've pulled up on top of the saddle and the girth stays put.

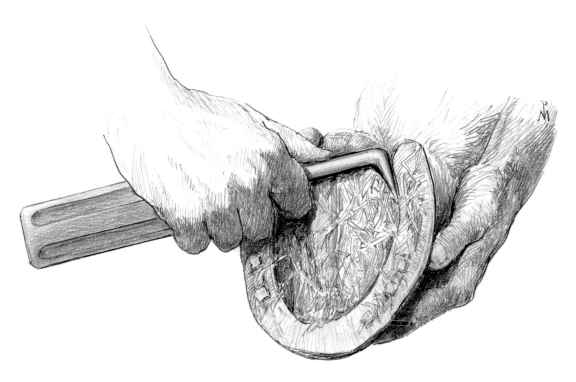

Screwdriver Hoof Pick

My hoof picks are constantly disappearing. I've had to buy many new ones after mine vanish after they've been left on the floor of the stall. So I decided to make my own using an old flat head screwdriver. I simply bent it gently into a right angle using a vise. I now have a perfectly serviceable hoof pick that didn't cost a cent!

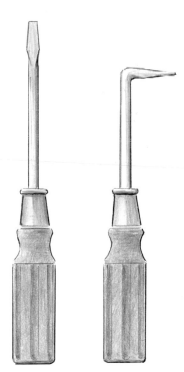

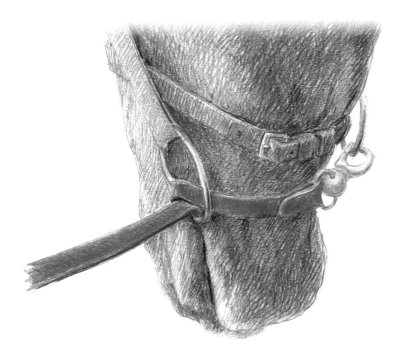

A RAINCOAT FOR MY SADDLE

Every rider knows how unpleasant it is to sit on a wet saddle when it's raining or snowing. Just going from the stable to the indoor arena is enough to get the seat soaked. So I made a waterproof saddle protector using an old child-sized windbreaker. I cut off the sleeves and threaded the stirrups through the holes to keep the jacket in place. Now my saddle has a raincoat! I just remove it before mounting my horse and my pants stay dry.

A Softer Curb Chain

When I use a lunge on my horse, I usually clip it on to the outer ring of the curb chain after threading it through the inner ring. This gives me better control when my horse is a little defiant. To soften the impact on the horse's sensitive chin groove, I loop the lunge twice around the inner ring. This makes the curb chain softer and the weight of the lunge doesn't rest on my horse's chin.

MAKESHIFT HALTER

I often forget my halter, so I sometimes just use a lunge to go fetch my mare from the field. I learned to make a spare halter using a series of loops in the lunge. The first loop goes around the neck, the second loop creates the cheek pieces and the third loop creates the noseband. I can catch my mare in a few seconds flat and bring her back to her stall!

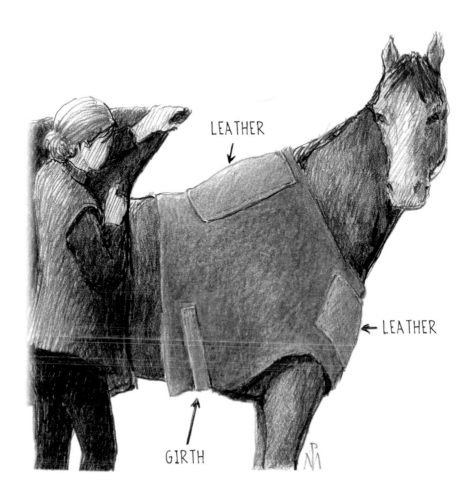

 # Custom Shoulder Guard

My aging horse has lost a lot of muscle mass this past year. Since his blankets have grown too big for him, the straps aren't secure anymore and end up hurting him. To keep him warm at night, I made him a fleece shoulder guard with leather reinforcements at the withers to evenly distribute the blanket's weight and two more patches on the shoulders. I added an adjustable girth around the chest and Velcro strips at the front to make the shoulder guard easy to slip on. Lastly, I place the blanket on top.

Check Your Saddle

I have a handy way to know whether your saddle is sitting in the right place and isn't hampering your horse's withers or spine. Using chalk of a different color than your horse's coat, color the underside of the saddle that sits on your horse. Place the saddle on his back in the correct mounting position. Mount your horse for a few minutes, ensure he is well aligned and standing on his four feet on even ground, and then gently dismount. The chalk will have transferred to your horse's back.

Saddlecloth Wear and Tear

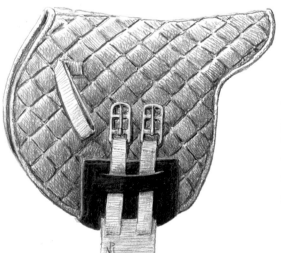

My saddlecloth always frays near the girth. So to prolong its life, I sewed a leather patch where the girth straps are tied. Then, using a knife, I made two small parallel cuts in the leather large enough to slide the girth straps through. Not only does this prevent wear and tear, but my saddlecloth stays firmly attached to my saddle.

A HANDY BUCKET HOLDER

Buckets don't last too long in stables: in no time at all they either crack or develop a hole. Instead of discarding them, I reuse them as bucket holders. I install them using a screw and a drill in the stalls that don't have feeding troughs. When I feed my horses, I just prepare each ration in a clean, intact bucket that I place inside a bucket holder. It makes feeding time more efficient!

BUFFING LEATHER IN THE SUMMER

In hot weather, solid leather grease tends to liquefy and become oily, making it much more difficult to apply with my usual rag. So I started using a paintbrush instead! With this tool, I can apply the oil evenly without making a mess, even in places the rag can't reach. It's also a handy method to restore old, worn-out leather.

Handmade Girth Sleeves

I'd had enough of my girth sleeves becoming worn out and damaged from mud and bad weather. Plus, they always slipped off. So I recycled an old pair of thick socks, cut off the feet and sewed the two pieces together. This girth sleeve is machine washable and didn't cost a cent; once it gets worn out, I just need another old pair of socks to replace it.

129

Nail Polish to the Rescue

My cat attacked my synthetic saddle and clawed holes in it near the edge of the cantle. I initially didn't think much of it, but a few weeks later I noticed that the holes had grown larger. I patched them with nail polish and now they're unnoticeable. To best conceal the damage, choose a clear polish or a shade that matches the color of the saddle.

WARM YOUR BIT

In the cold winter months, just before putting my horse's bridle on, I run the bit under hot water until the metal is warm and then dry it off. This way, my horse isn't taken by surprise and doesn't resist the bridle. Make sure to warm the bit just before using it, as it will cool very quickly.

KEEP YOUR TACK BAG DRY

I have an old halter that rusts when I store it in my tack bag. The bag traps the moisture on the halter, especially if my horse has been sweating. To solve this problem, I save the moisture absorbing packets that come with a new pair of shoes and leave one in my tack bag. For best results, replace the packets regularly.

Serviceable Suspenders

My horse's blanket straps often break when I leave his blanket on overnight. To avoid this, simply use ordinary suspenders and adjust them to fit your horse. Clip suspenders will hold the blanket in place around the horse's barrel. They can also be used around the horse's breast or under the belly or tail.

Secure Clasp

I often have trouble keeping my horse's blanket clasps closed. He takes mischievous delight in getting out of his blanket, which then gets trampled and torn. I found a solution to hold "T" clasps shut. Just close the clasp as you normally would and slide a rubber gasket (like the kind you would find on swing-top beer or lemonade bottles) onto the "T." The clasp will stay shut, even if your horse lies down or moves around. It's cheap and it works!

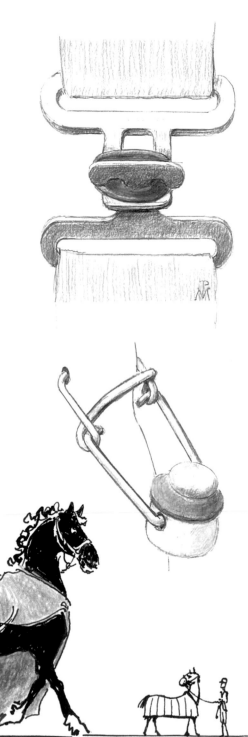

ESSENTIAL TIPS

FACILITIES

Homemade Crosscountry Obstacles

I live near a small forest where I can collect wood. To introduce my young horse to crosscountry jumping, I made an obstacle by bundling branches together, tying the bundles with twine or tape and stacking them one on top of the other to form a pyramid. One important detail: spread sand on the takeoff and landing of jumps since the grass in the pasture can be slippery.

You can also make obstacles out of old tires. To do so, you will need the following: about 10 tires, a fairly long obstacle rail, a round post you'll need to saw in two, boards and long nails.

Pass the obstacle rail through the tires, leaving some room at the ends. Make two wooden stands by nailing the round posts to the boards and attach the tire rail to the stands with the long nails. The obstacle is at the right height when the tires appear to be touching the ground.

Spread sand on the takeoff and landing of the obstacle for stable footing. The advantage of this jump is that the horse won't get hurt if he touches the tires.

I planted dogwood, an incredibly fast-growing shrub normally used as a hedge because it produces a thick bush, in some small baskets. After a few months, I pruned the shrubs and lined them up behind a 20 inch (50 cm) long fence used to keep them upright. If you don't have a hedge, you can use straw brooms like the kind that are used in stables. To increase the difficulty of the jump, I created a river in front of the hedge using a tarp anchored by two obstacle rails. At first, my horse found the obstacle a bit daunting, but he now jumps it with ease.

I build my own obstacles since my horses live at home and there aren't any crosscountry facilities nearby. I salvaged blue plastic storage drums and laid them end to end on their sides to create a large visible obstacle that can be easily jumped. Before positioning the drums, I spread sand over a large area, including the takeoff and landing, and also poured sand inside the drums to weigh them down. Lastly, I wedged rocks under the ends of the drums so they wouldn't roll.

I made a second obstacle with eight bales of straw. The advantage of using bales is that the size and shape of the obstacle can easily be changed. Plus, bales will stay where you put them and won't hurt the horse if he touches them while in flight. I usually stack them in a U shape to form a skinny, which encourages my horse to jump directly over the center. I also spread some sand on the takeoff and landing. Easy!

Since I don't have the means to build obstacles, I use sandbags available from a nearby building company that I pile in staggered rows to create a stable obstacle. The good thing about using sandbags is that I can change the height of the obstacle to fit the needs of each session. To avoid slipping on takeoff and landing, I spread a thick layer of sand 3 feet (1 m) in front of the obstacle and 5 feet (1.5 m) behind it.

"HOMEMADE" OBSTACLE

I built a small ring on my property so I would have a place to ride my horse and practice jumping just for fun. So I looked for a way to build an inexpensive obstacle that meets all the safety requirements. I bought clear plastic jugs, filled them with water (you can add food coloring to create colorful containers) and stacked them on their sides. You now have a decorative obstacle that is flexible and safe, and one you can easily customize to your liking!

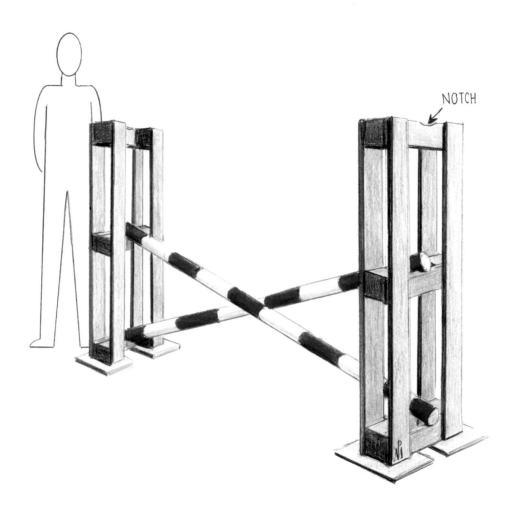

NOTCH

 # Homemade Standards

Even though I'm not a huge fan of show jumping, I still enjoy jumping a few rails once in a while with my 7-year-old Haflinger, so I built my own standards that are not only inexpensive, but also lighter than traditional standards. I salvaged pallets that I cut in half lengthwise and reinforced the base by creating feet out of reclaimed boards for more stability. I made small notches in the wood with a sander to hold the rails in place but still allow freedom of movement if my horse bumps them. If need be, you can place sandbags on the feet to weigh them down.

HAY ON DEMAND

I wanted to build a hayrack or hang a haynet so hay would always be available in my horse's stall without it being directly on the ground. So I invented a very practical hay feeder using an old truck tire that I cut along its circumference (this is the most tedious part). Since there are metal cords in the tire, I covered the cut edge with plastic tubing, which I split lengthwise and screwed onto the rubber. I then set a plastic basin with the same diameter as the tire inside the tire and used chains to hang my contraption from the stable ceiling. This very solid setup has the advantage of acting like a traffic circle: the horses walk around it so it can't get wedged in a corner and the dominant horse can't prevent his fellow horse from eating. Sweeping is also much easier now!

Another inexpensive way that I keep my horse's hay off the ground is by using a crate that I got from a roofer for roofing slates. After removing all the sharp edges, I reinforced the crate with pieces of wood and placed the crate in the pasture shelter. My horses can come and go as they please and eat their hay in peace.

Simple Standards

It's fun to practice obstacle courses, but it's quite the chore hauling standards around to set up jumps in the arena. I simplified this task by designing a rail support that is much easier to move. It consists of building a small ladder with wide rungs for holding the rail using two furring strips and small boards. Once built, lean this support wherever you want against the parapet of the arena.

AN ORIGINAL BRIDLE HOLDER

Don't throw out your used horseshoes; turn them into a D.I.Y. project! Horseshoes make excellent tack room hooks for halters and bridles. Use a grinder to cut a horseshoe in half then weld one half perpendicularly onto a full horseshoe. For the finishing touch, paint your new hook black.

A Practical Basketball Net

I take care of several horses and needed a sturdy haynet that I could easily fill from outside the stall. So I recycled our old basketball net. I detached the backboard but kept the rim and drilled it to the stall wall. Now I have a super practical haynet!

ANTI-POOP

NO POOPING
IN THE TROUGH

My horse has an infuriating habit of defecating in his feeding trough, which is located in the corner of his stall. After giving it some thought, I came up with the idea of installing a metal bar about 12 inches (30 cm) in front of the trough. I made a hole in the walls on either side of the trough, slid the bar in the holes and mortared it in place. Now my horse's backside can't get near his feeding trough and he's found another corner of the stall to do his business!

A CONVERTED WARDROBE

I wanted a place to store my tack away from dust, rodents and other country inconveniences, so I salvaged an old wardrobe from my uncle's garage. It already has a shelf that I use for storing medication, bottles and treats, and a rod that is perfect for hanging saddlecloths. I screwed empty tin cans upright on the left sidewall to hold items like paint brushes, salves and hoof picks. A magazine holder fastened above the cans houses sponges, combs and brushes. On the left-hand side of the back wall, I attached a coat rack for halters, lunges and bridles. Next to the coat rack, I screwed in two shelf brackets to use as a saddle rack. I nailed two more coat racks on the right sidewall for my stirrup leathers. The cost: around $10.

HOSE HOLDER

I set up a shower along the side of the stable, but I often tripped over the long hose that was always dragging on the ground. That all changed one day when I realized that a car wheel was the solution to my problem. I removed the tire and fastened the metal rim to the stable wall to make the ideal spool. And in one fell swoop, the hose is neatly stored!

A TIDY TACK ROOM

I built a small tack room next to my horse stalls, but since there isn't a lot of space and I'm not very handy with tools, I decided not to install shelves. I did, however, find a simple, lowcost solution for keeping my tack room tidy. I hammered some long nails into the wooden walls and linked them together with baler twine. The nails can hold items like my riding helmet, bell boots and bridle, and the twine can easily support my saddlecloth and girth sleeve.

 # Awning Storage

My horse shelter is not very big so I need clever space-saving solutions for storing straw. (I first checked with my insurance company before making this change to my horse's abode.) I turned the awning of the stalls into storage space for straw bales by nailing wooden slats to the roof framing. The space between each slat should be narrower than the length of the bales (or the width, depending on the chosen arrangement). I can easily use a pitchfork to put up or bring down the bales. The straw is stored neatly in a dry place and I've saved space!

STORAGE IDEA

I wanted an inexpensive saddle rack that could be padlocked and enclosed to keep out the dust and that I could customize and modify to meet my wants and needs. I salvaged a lidded trash can and made an opening in the lower front part. I fastened two hinges onto the cutout to be able to open and close this "door" and installed two hasps that can be padlocked. Above the opening on the inside of the trash can, I installed a saddle rack and two bridle hooks to hold my bridle, halter and saddle. (I have a dressage saddle, but there would be enough room to store an all-purpose saddle, a show jumping saddle, an endurance saddle or a TREC (Techniques de Rondonee Equestre de Competition) saddle; however, a western or Portuguese saddle would be too wide.) In the bottom of the trash can, I store my grooming box, saddlecloth, shin boots, bell boots ... all the basic riding gear. I painted the lid metallic blue and the rest black. It's a rather unique trunk that became a hit in my stable!

Clever Hitch System

When I go riding, I sometimes have to hitch my horse for long periods when I stop to eat, so I invented a system to avoid lunge entanglements. I hang a pulley from a high sturdy tree branch and pass a short length of rope weighted down with a piece of wood through the pulley. I make a loop on the other end of the rope and thread the lunge through before tying the lunge to the tree trunk. The lunge doesn't drag on the ground and my horse can still move freely.

143

Tire Changes

When I need to change a flat tire on my two-horse trailer, I use a beveled wood wheel chock to elevate the trailer (a beam would also do the trick). The top part that holds the supporting wheel must be at least 16 inches (40 cm) long and the bottom part that rests on the ground should be at least 32 inches (80 cm) long. The wheel chock must be at least 4 inches (10 cm) wide to hold the weight of the trailer.

Two-horse trailers generally have two wheels per side, so I lift the trailer by propping up the good tire. I use a wrench to unscrew the nuts on the flat tire, position the beveled end of the chock in front of the good tire and get someone to guide me as I maneuver the trailer onto the chock. With the flat tire now turning freely, I simply remove it and replace it with a spare tire like I would to change a car tire.

I customized my wheel chock with a groove on top to immobilize the supporting wheel. You don't compromise when safety is concerned.

My Houdini Horse

My little rascal of a horse has an infuriating habit of escaping from his stall whenever he pleases. He has figured out a way of nudging the door latch with his teeth and sliding it open with his lips. The next thing you know, he's outside! I don't want to barricade the door because I still want to be able to open it quickly and easily.

To solve my problem, I fastened another latch vertically behind the stall door latch. Now when my horse plays with his door latch, he can no longer slide it open because it's blocked by the vertical latch. To open the stall door, I first lift the vertical latch then slide open the horizontal latch. Easy!

Another option is to install a second door latch below the original latch, low enough so the horse can't reach it. The horse can still play with the top latch but can't escape!

BLANKET HANGER

I never know where to put my horse's winter blanket after removing it to get him ready for a ride. The floor in the stable or stall is not always the cleanest and since my horse tends to chew on things, I didn't want to leave the blanket on his door or in his trough. So I came up with the idea of installing two tie rings on the stable wall next to my horse's stall. I tied both ends of a rope securely to the rings and made sure it stayed taut. Now I can hang my horse's blanket and saddlecloth on the rope. However, be aware that this setup isn't strong enough to hold the weight of a saddle.

A NEW HAYRACK

When my hayrack broke, I built a new one without breaking the bank using a donated pedestrian barricade. I attached the barricade to the wall with chains (rope would suffice) and slanted it like a hayrack, placing the feet against the wall so they wouldn't injure my horse. An even simpler solution is to make a hayrack out of a wooden ladder!

Roll Out the Red Carpet

Loading my horse into the trailer has always been very stressful because my horse becomes frightened and uncooperative when he hears the sound of his hooves on the ramp. To ease his fears, I cover the ramp with an old carpet starting on the ground far enough in front of the ramp and ending inside the trailer. My horse can no longer tell the difference between solid ground and the trailer and isn't scared of walking on the ramp, which now makes less noise. Loading my horse into the trailer is now a walk in the park.

Horseshoe Hooks

I get a farrier to shoe my two horses and have amassed a large collection of horseshoes since I never throw anything out. So I transformed some of them into tack hooks to hold my riding helmet, halter, etc. After cleaning and scraping them, I covered them with a rustproofing compound and nailed them by the shoe branch to a wooden beam. Very practical!

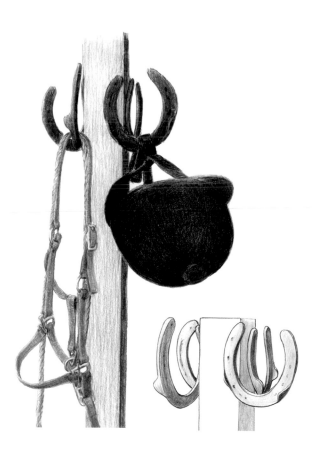

HOMEMADE JUMPS

I built a small ring on my property so I would have a place to ride my horse and practice jumping just for fun. I scour the countryside in search of anything I can use to build inexpensive obstacles that meet all the safety requirements. I can make adequate jumps out of items I collect like used barrels from grape growers, fallen branches scavenged in the forest and square bales of straw. Most equine clubs recycle objects and have no shortage of ideas. Some use old canoes placed upside down on rails to make fun and colorful obstacles.

COMFORT FOR PAWING HORSES

Some horses have a nasty habit of pawing the ground in front of their stall door, which leads to premature wear on their shoes and possible injury. To prevent pawing, lay a half-inch (1 cm) thick rubber mat on the ground to cover the entire width of the stall door. Start by thoroughly scraping and cleaning the concrete floor and then cover the underside of the mat with contact adhesive before anchoring it to the ground with bolts spaced 8 to 12 inches (20 to 30 cm) apart. Guaranteed success! Besides, most horses stop pawing as soon as they feel the rubber.

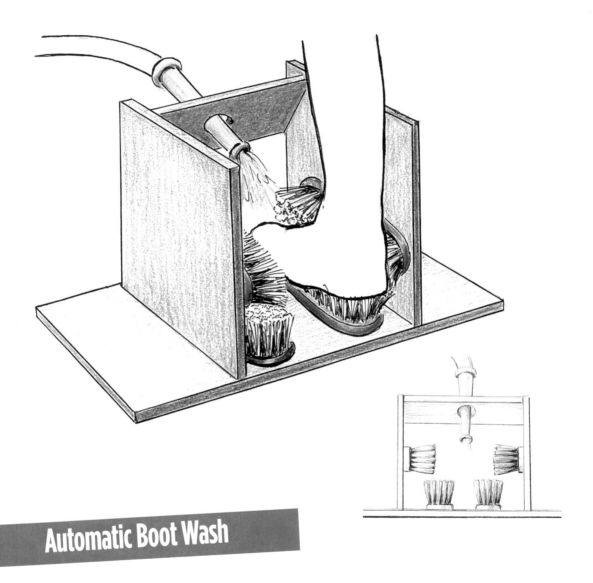

Automatic Boot Wash

Cleaning my boots covered in dirt, mud and manure after mucking out horse stalls is a real chore because I first have to hunt down my boot brushes before scrubbing my boots and rinsing them off with water. So I decided to build an "automatic boot wash" out of four recycled boards and four used dandy brushes. I screwed the brushes into the boards and cut a hole in one of the boards to pass a garden hose through. Since I invented this small "brush box," cleaning our boots is fun for the entire family!

Tin Can Storage

I have a hard time keeping my grooming supplies and bandages organized for longer than 2 weeks in my tiny tack room. So I decided to optimize my storage space by fastening large tin cans horizontally and vertically to a partition.

Before starting I made sure there weren't any sharp edges on the cans. Then I used a hammer and nail to carefully punch a hole in each can through which I slid an L-shaped nail that I used to fasten the cans to the wall (or any wood surface). All that's left to do is to fill them with my supplies.

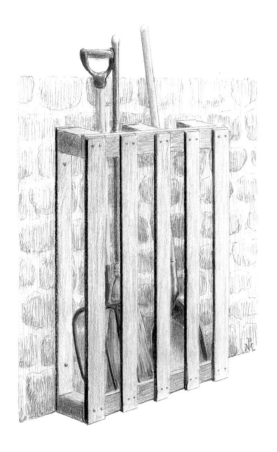

Everything in its Place

I don't have storage space for my stable cleaning supplies so brooms, pitchforks and shovels always seem to get left lying around the stable. It's not only annoying having to search high and low for them when it's time to muck out stalls or sweep the alley, but it's also a tripping hazard for humans and horses. So I came up with a simple storage solution that keeps everything accessible in one spot and creates a safer environment. I salvaged a wood pallet measuring 3 feet x 4 feet (1 m x 1.20 m) and stood it against the wall to hold long-handled tools when they're not in use. The wood pallet is lightweight yet sturdy and can easily be converted to meet your needs. And if one of the boards gets damaged, it can be easily repaired with a hammer and nails.

AUTOMATIC FEEDER

An automatic feeder is ideal for horse owners with staggered work schedules or who plan to be away during feeding time because it allows horses to eat at their usual time even if their owners are away or running late! Any handyman can set up this device by simply connecting a drop door feeder to an electric automatic timer. Fill the feeder with hay at night and it will drop hay into the horse's stall at the set time the next morning (7 a.m., let's say). With this practical device, you can go for an early morning ride without having to get up at the crack of dawn to feed your horse and wait for him to digest his food.

A Clever Feed Storage Bin Solution

A feed storage bin is equipped with a heavy lid that a horse can't lift open with its nose, but it can also be problematic for humans because having to hold up a heavy lid with one arm while scooping out 20 rations isn't very practical. So I set up a counterweight system using old horseshoes, two ropes and two pulleys mounted on the wall. One end of each rope is connected to the bin lid while the other end holds old horseshoes as counterweights. The ropes slide through the pulleys when you lift the lid and the counterweights hold the bin lid open. Now I can easily divvy up rations.

My Horse is a Puller

My Mérens has a bad habit of pulling back when tied. He even broke a brand new "anti-pull" lunge the first time I used it on him. He recently pulled back twice while I was removing his bridle so I made an elastic lunge out of a very large truck tire inner tube. When my horse decided to pull back, he was surprised that the lunge wasn't as stiff as usual.

Never stand behind your horse and whip him to get him to move forward. This is dangerous and won't solve the problem. If you want to make your horse understand that pulling is useless, try the sandbag method.

First find a wide open space like a paddock that is void of hazards such as standards and obstacle rails that could injure your horse. Fit your horse with a sturdy halter. Attach one end of a lunge line to the halter and the other end to a large sandbag or grain bag weighing at least 110 pounds (50 kg) and positioned in the middle of the paddock. Move out of the way because your horse will no doubt pull back at first. After a while, the horse will realize that staying calm is less tiring than dragging around such a heavy weight. Repeat this exercise daily until your horse stops pulling.

A horse that pulls back when tied is always very worrisome because the lunge could break, which could cause the horse to fall backwards. Everyone uses a different tactic to suppress this bad reflex. In my case, instead of tying the lunge directly to a wall ring, I tie it to a hookless bungee cord and fasten the bungee cord to a wall ring. Now when my horse pulls back, the bungee cord provides some give and prevents the lunge from breaking. The horse gets confused when he doesn't feel resistance, so he stops pulling back.

HANDY RIDING TACK BOX

I needed a box to store my riding tack in the car, so I decided to make one. Using ¾ inch (10 mm) thick plywood, I cut two 24 inch x 14 inch (60 x 35 cm) boards for the long sides, one 16 inch x 24 inch (42 x 60 cm) piece for the bottom and two 16 inch x 14 inch (42 x 35 cm) boards for the short sides. I assembled the box using 24 screws or nails. I glued a plank and a bar together to create a sturdy saddle holder. Finally, I drilled two holes on each side of the box to thread cords to use as handles.

RUNAWAY PONY

The pony I ride manages to unlatch his door and escape from his stall. While waiting for his owner to install a second latch on the bottom of the stall door, I came up with a simple way to keep him from running away when it's my turn to look after him. Since I always have a lunge on hand, I simply attach a lunge snap hook onto the latch to secure it. The lunge can easily be hooked onto a ring or left hanging on the door.

Hay Insulation

When the temperature dips below zero, our stable goes into panic mode. We can't fill the drinking troughs because our outdoor taps are frozen. So when the weather forecast predicts cold temperatures, I insulate the taps with a bale of hay. I cut an opening in the bale just large enough to fit around the faucet and I place it snug against the wall.

Sliding Gate

My pony broke his pasture door while horsing around with another horse. Gate maintenance in pastures, arenas and paddocks is never-ending. Horses' antics added to regular wear and tear take their toll; as a result, boards and gates often need replacement. So I came up with a sturdy solution: a sliding gate.

I attached the heel of some old horseshoes to the gate's pillars using lag bolts from the hardware store, thereby creating sturdy "loops." I then simply slid round posts through them to create a barrier. It is harder for the horses to break the gate by leaning on it and you can slide it open to enter into the pasture wherever you want. Nifty!

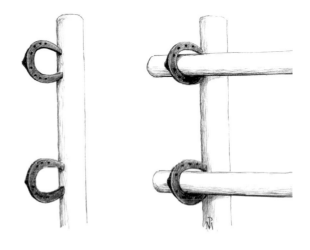

FLIES, BE GONE!

To protect my horses from pesky flies, I installed sticky fly paper on the ceiling of their shelter in the pasture. Make sure to attach both ends of the paper to the ceiling using thumbtacks or transparent adhesive tape; otherwise, it could stick to the horses if you leave it hanging. Do, however, let it dangle a bit. For best results, hang some in all four corners of the shelter.

Self-Serve Hayrack

My horses' hayrack had started to crumble so I had to replace it on a tight budget. I made a square rack using 16 wooden poles each measuring nearly 6 feet (2 m). I stacked the poles four high on each side and drilled holes through each pole 12 inches (30 cm) from each end. To solidify my construction, I inserted rebar through the holes right into the ground so it wouldn't stick out. You can also add poles in the center of the rack for support to keep the hay from falling on the ground. Since I don't need to move my hayrack, I picked an area of the pasture that was elevated and sheltered to avoid pools of stagnant rain water.

Jumbo Hayrack

My horses live in loose housing and I use 880 pound (400 kg) bundles of hay that don't fit in regular feeders. So I made my own hayrack to distribute hay to my horses.

I needed the hayrack to be easily accessible by tractor, so I used the walls of my barn (to protect the feeder from the elements) and built a large rack out of recycled pallets. I used three pallets to make a wall-to-wall base to keep the hay off the damp ground. I made the ends of the rack using pallets placed vertically across the width of the base. I hammered more pallets along the length of the base, with one of the sides slightly lower to ensure my ponies can easily reach the hay. All that's left to do is deposit the 880 pound (400 kg) bundle of hay in my homemade hayrack with my tractor. With this setup, it's much easier to distribute the hay and much less of it goes to waste.

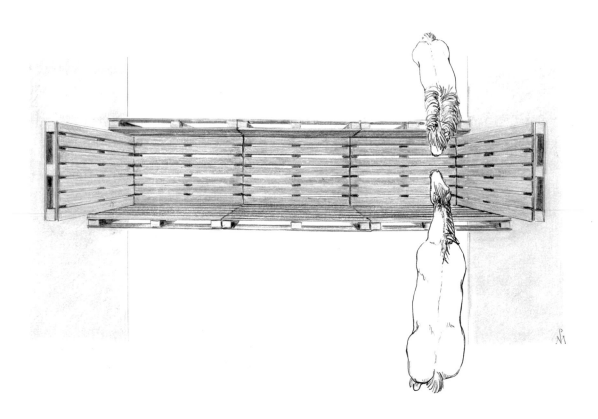

SPARE HANDLE

I installed an electric fence around my horse's pasture. Having many openings around the fence is practical, depending on the area of the pasture you want to access, but often there aren't enough insulated handles to avoid electric shocks. So I made a spare handle using a 16 ounce (500 ml) plastic soda bottle and a bit of metal from a coat hanger. Simply make holes in the bottom of the bottle to run the electric wire through and a hole in the cap for the piece of metal. Bend the metal from the hanger so it hooks easily onto the fence post.

A Modern Hayrack

My horse lives in a large stall next to my house. I wanted to use a feeding rack for his hay but since he likes to chew on wood, a wooden hayrack was out of the question. So, I cut the legs off an old safety gate using a hacksaw. I then installed two brackets on one of the walls in the stall to hang the bottom of the gate and two rings linked to chains attached to the top of the gate. I now have a foldable hayrack that stands up to my horse's chewing habits!

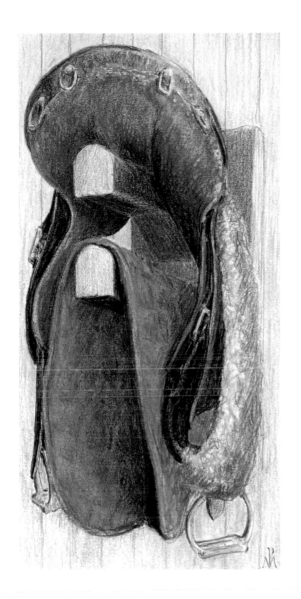

Saddlecloth Drying Rack

In my riding center's tack room, we used to drape our saddlecloths over our saddles after a ride. But they didn't dry very well this way or they'd end up on the ground, which wasn't very pleasant for the next rider. So I added a bar under each saddle to hang the saddlecloth after a ride. This way, the cloths dry faster and everything looks tidier.

NIFTY LOCKER

I needed a locker to store all my small riding tack, so I reclaimed an old refrigerator that no longer worked. I stored my grease pots, tar pots and first aid kit inside the door and put my saddlecloths, grooming box and riding helmet on the shelves. I added adhesive hooks on the sides to hang my bits. This nifty, one-of-a-kind locker keeps my tack dry. Luckily I don't have to move it very often.

 # Lowcost Lunging Ring

I built a 50 foot (15 m) diameter lunging ring in a corner of my pasture using PVC fence posts, electrical ribbon, small bottles and sand mixed with soil. I marked the perimeter of my ring and installed the posts and then ran the ribbon along the posts. I filled the bottles with water to make them heavier and lined them up one beside the other around the ring to create a border. Finally, I spread a layer of sand in the center and my ring was ready to use.

TACK ROOM TIPS!

I put together a small tack room in my house. I hammered horseshoes into a wooden board on the wall to hang my equipment, attached baler twine directly onto the wood panelling to hang my saddlecloths and used a pallet to make a tool rack. This rack doubles as a memo board that I check before I go out to the pasture to ride my horses. On it I wrote the basic necessities for a horseback ride. Now, I never forget anything and don't have to put out a desperate call for someone to bring me the one item I left behind!

Windproof Door

My horses live in a very open pasture that doesn't have many trees. Their shelter gets them out of the rain but it does little to protect them against the wind or insects. So I installed a PVC strip curtain like the ones used in warehouses, which I hung using hooks on a rail. The only drawback is getting your horses used to going through the curtain without getting spooked.

Lock Up Your Horses!

My horse managed to break his door latch after fiddling with it repeatedly. I had to find a quick fix to keep him from escaping while waiting to repair the latch. I simply slid a horseshoe into the metal fastener that the latch usually sits in. My horse can't open the door and it's quite an elegant solution.

RIDING

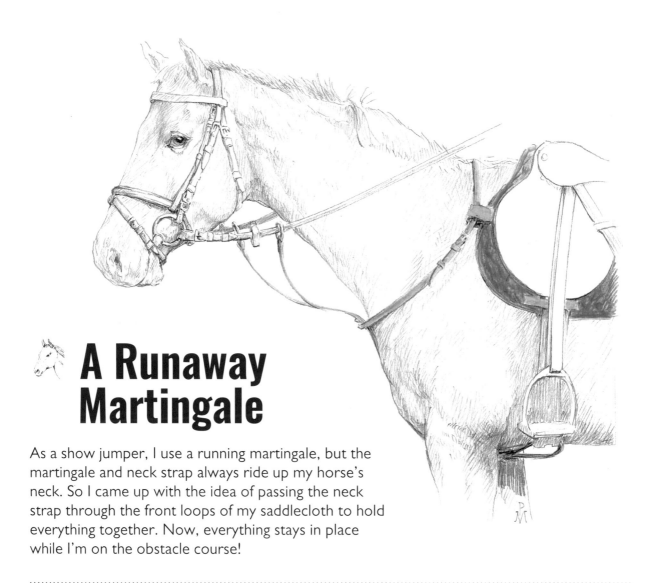

A Runaway Martingale

As a show jumper, I use a running martingale, but the martingale and neck strap always ride up my horse's neck. So I came up with the idea of passing the neck strap through the front loops of my saddlecloth to hold everything together. Now, everything stays in place while I'm on the obstacle course!

PROTECTIVE PETROLEUM JELLY

On a crosscountry course, a horse can get scratched by the slightest contact with a solid fence. So as an event rider, I coat my horse's legs with petroleum jelly. This way, if his legs touch a fence, the petroleum jelly helps them slide over more easily. No more bumps or scrapes! I prefer using white petroleum jelly because it's easier to remove afterwards. I rub it on the front of my horse's legs from top to bottom, shin boots, bell boots and all. Here's another useful tip: put the bridle on last to avoid getting petroleum jelly on the reins, which can result in slippery hands!

Seesaw Fence

The principle of the seesaw fence was invented by Jacques Pécout, track superintendent. This is how it's made. The goal is to build a liverpool or small gate-type obstacle that allows the rider to tackle a series of jumps without having to dismount every time the fence is knocked over. The fence must stand back up on its own and be easy to move. A seesaw fence is a narrow obstacle (about 5 feet or 1.5 m wide, front view) with the lowest possible center of gravity and the heaviest possible base. See the drawing for the optimal dimensions. Make the base and bottom rail out of oak or any other type of heavy wood and use pine to build the gate itself. You can also customize your obstacle by dressing it up.

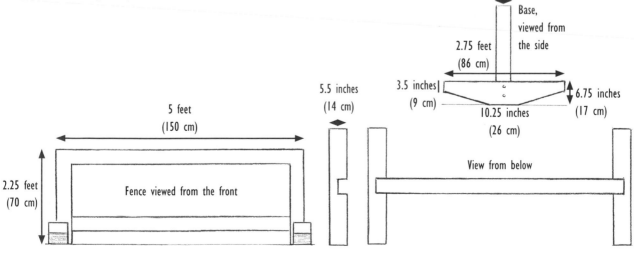

4 inches
(10 cm)

Base, viewed from the side

2.75 feet
(86 cm)

3.5 inches
(9 cm)

10.25 inches
(26 cm)

6.75 inches
(17 cm)

5 feet
(150 cm)

5.5 inches
(14 cm)

2.25 feet
(70 cm)

Fence viewed from the front

View from below

NOISY BOOTS

There's nothing more dangerous outside or inside an arena than a horse spooked by the sound of a plastic bag. To get my Anglo-Arabian used to this sort of rustling sound, I wore plastic bags for 2 weeks over my boots like slippers while grooming him. By hearing me regularly make a swishing noise beside him, he is now accustomed to the sound.

 # A Tarp Serving Tray

I regularly take part in qualification contests for hobby and recreational horses. My young horses need to be ready for anything including walking on tarps, which some horses take to more easily than others. So I train them at home by scattering treats over a tarp. Apples, carrots, pieces of dry bread … all of their favorites await. In general, it's stomach over mind.

Adjusted Stirrups

Whenever I used someone else's saddle, I always had trouble adjusting the stirrups to the correct length. I often ended up adjusting them three or four times without ever finding the right length. I solved this problem once and for all by unbuckling the stirrup leathers and stirrups from my own saddle and buckling them to the borrowed saddle. Since the straps are already adjusted for my height, I'm no longer shaky when I sit in the saddle.

Another tip: the length of the stirrup leathers depends on the discipline (jumping, dressage, trail riding, etc.). The bar of the stirrup should be level with your ankle bone when your leg is hanging relaxed down the horse's side. Set the length to match your physique, riding habits and discipline (as a general rule, one or two holes shorter for jumping and outdoor activities).

A Firm Grip

Since the mushroom on my crop isn't very prominent, the crop often slips through my fingers, which forces me to dismount to retrieve it when I'm riding alone in the ring. I find that putting my hand through the wrist loop isn't the safest: in case of a fall, the crop can catch on something and cause an injury.

My solution for preventing my crop from slipping out of my hand is to place a leather rein stop just below the crop mushroom. You can buy individual rein stops from any saddler. I no longer spend time dismounting to pick up my crop!

USEFUL POLO GEAR

I would braid my horse's tail the day before a competition to save time on show day; however, I would often find that my horse had undone the braid when he rolled around on the ground during the night. To avoid having to re-braid his tail in the morning, I now wrap polo bandages around the braid at night. When I load my horse into the trailer the next day, the braid is intact and I'm not rushing to get to the competition.

EASY SADDLE HOLDER

Instead of leaving my saddle on the ground, I rig up a makeshift saddle holder out of baler twine and a stick (or a branch picked up on the event grounds). I tie one end of the twine around the center of the stick and the other end to the stall bars or another solid support. To hold my saddle, all I have to do is place the saddle flaps perpendicularly on the stick.

We can trot thanks to NON-SLIP ANTIFREEZE

Nonslip Horseshoes

I enjoy going riding even during the winter, but small clumps of snow build up under my horse's hooves when the roads are snowy, making it difficult for him to walk correctly. When this happens, I'm afraid he might slip.

I found a creative solution: I spray my horse's shoes and soles with antifreeze in an aerosol container. I can now trot without risking a fall! I do however have to bring the container with me in my saddle bag since I have to reapply the antifreeze about every half hour.

Pockets Everywhere

When I go riding I bring along certain things like my car keys, papers, sunglasses, some carrots, a hoof pick (to remove stones wedged under hooves) and a small bottle of water. Riding trousers don't have big enough pockets to store everything in and I don't wear a jacket during the summer. Saddlecloth pockets aren't always big enough to store necessities snugly and items clang together loudly. My solution was to sew pockets with sturdy fabric onto my saddlecloth, with each individual pocket made to fit a specific item. I sewed a Velcro strip under each flap to close the pockets. Lastly, I put a plastic liner in the pockets meant for my papers and cell phone to protect them from bad weather and horse sweat. Each item has its place.

VELCRO

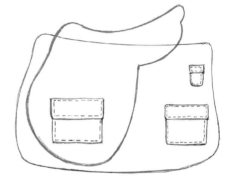

Our pockets are full

Hidden wallet pocket
(under the saddle flap)

Carrot pocket

Key pocket
and sunglasses pocket

Beverage pocket

Memory Aid

I have trouble memorizing obstacle courses. Even when I go over them in my head, concentrate very hard or watch other competitors, nothing seems to work. To overcome this frustrating problem during competitions, I use mnemonics to jog my memory. I walk the course first with my coach, then alone. Every time I walk past an obstacle, I associate its color, appearance and liverpool with animals, locations or even famous monuments. I then sit near the course and repeat several times out loud the "names" of the obstacles until I know them by heart. I haven't made any mistakes since I started using this trick!

Memorizing Arena Letters

I regularly take part in dressage competitions, but I have a very hard time remembering the letters around the arena, which makes it difficult to perform an accurate dressage test; however, I have found some sayings to use as memory aids. There are 12 visible letters on the outside edge of the arena and 5 invisible letters along the center line from A (entrance) to C (judges), which makes a total of 17 letters. For the outside letters AKVESHCMRBPF (clockwise), the saying is All King Victor's Expensive Show Horses Can Make Really Big Pongy Farts. For the invisible line DLXIG, the saying is Doing Lots Xtra Is Good.

WELL-FASTENED POLO BANDAGES

Since I work my horse outside, my polo bandages are subjected to mud, bad weather and a lot of use, and so the fasteners on the bandages quickly lose their adhesiveness. Since the bandages are still in good shape, I extend their life with a tailor-made solution: once the bandage is on the horse, I reinforce the fastener with thin super-resistant tape sold at supermarkets and hardware stores.

Stirrup Leather Guard

One stirrup bar safety latch no longer stays closed on my saddle. Consequently, when I ride uphill, the stirrup leather slips off and falls to the ground! It's not very safe and I have to dismount to retrieve my stirrup leather and stirrup. To avoid this sort of headache, I fasten a leather strap to the ring on the front of my saddle, and then attach the stirrup leather to the leather strap. Now if the safety latch opens, the stirrup leather stays connected to the saddle by the leather strap, and I no longer have to dismount!

Movable Arena Letters

To make solid, weather-resistant arena letters, I used three iron rods, two of the same length and one shorter one, and I welded the ends together to form a three-sided rectangle. Then I cut a piece of thin sheet metal the same width as my rectangle and welded it to the frame. This is where the letter goes. Lastly, I added a metal plate to reinforce the bottom of the letter holder. For the letter itself, I made a cardboard stencil, taped it to the sheet metal and colored it in using a smear-proof black marker. I repeated the same procedure for all the arena letters, which I stuck in the sand around my ring.

A HIDING PLACE FOR TREATS

I always use treats when trying to teach my pony something new, but the mere smell of a treat drives him to distraction and makes him hard to handle. So now I stick the treat inside my sock. My pony can't smell the treat as much and stays focused, yet the treat is within reach and I can reward him when he does what I ask, with both hands free.

 # Comfortable Bareback Riding

Riding bareback can be quite the ordeal if your horse's withers and back are uncomfortable. In order for my horse to keep his freedom of movement and for me to sit comfortably, I reinforced an old thick saddlecloth with a piece of foam where is sits on my horse's withers. I then used sewing thread to sew two casings for the girth a third of the way from each edge of the saddlecloth. To make the casings, make openings along the seams for the girth straps to stick out of and measure the width of the two stirrup leathers you want to use. Use chalk to mark the casings and then sew stitches on either side. Pass the straps through the casings and attach a girth. Now when I feel like riding bareback, I just have to put the saddlecloth on my horse's back and fasten the girth. There's nothing like comfort!

BY THE LETTER

I built a ring on my property to work my horse and wanted to install letters on the rails. I came up with a way of doing so without spending a fortune on store-bought letters. I collected twelve plastic covers from large round drums of laundry detergent (or plastic tubs of dry dog food). Using a colored marker, I traced one letter per cover. Then I nailed these covers to the wooden rails of my ring.

Another trick is to make your own wooden letters. I salvaged a large wooden board that was once used as a shelf, stripped it and cut it into 12 squares 4 inch x 6 inch (10 cm x 15 cm). Then I engraved the shape of the letters into the wood and filled the grooves with bright paint to show the letters off. They're lovely, practical, decorative and cost-effective!

Western Reins

I use leather western split reins (without a buckle) that are way too long. They're very awkward, but I'm not sure if I should cut them.

A technique that works well if the reins are too long is to tape them together. To do so, I "bridged" the reins at the desired length (the reins cross, the left hand holds the left rein and the excess from the right rein and vice-versa for the right hand), then I wrapped tape around several areas of the overlapping section. The drawback is that the adhesive from the tape can leave unsightly marks on leather reins. To avoid this problem, you could also make about six leather loops to tie the reins together, but tape is much more practical.

WESTERN SADLE

My western saddle is the very definition of uncomfortable, so I decided to buffer it with a saddle pad. I centered the saddle pad over the seat of the saddle and glued it in place. To make it look nice, I bought a sheepskin western saddle cover and placed it over the pad. I finally have a comfortable saddle that didn't cost much!

Allseason Hooves

I love going riding, but winter can be hard on my horse because snow accumulates under his hooves and he risks twisting a hoof or falling. My solution for preventing snow buildup is to smear a generous amount of lard on his shoes and soles. When we're out all day, I reapply a second layer around midday. No more slipping!

MOUNTING

When practicing mounting my horse, my instructor asks me to let go of the reins, but they slide forward along my horse's neck right up to his ears. The reins bother him and risk getting stepped on. To avoid this problem, I came up with the idea of sliding the reins through the front loops of the saddlecloth. The reins now stay put and if I have to grab them quickly, the Velcro on the loops unfastens easily. I can calmly go about doing my exercises!

NO PANICKING

Some horses are very nervous and enter their stall like a tornado, crashing into their rider who risks getting knocked against the doorjamb. To prevent this from happening, place a layer of straw in front of the doorway. The horse will naturally lower his head to sniff at the straw that's blocking the entrance to his stall. He'll then enter at a leisurely pace. Repeat this procedure while gradually decreasing the amount of straw used.

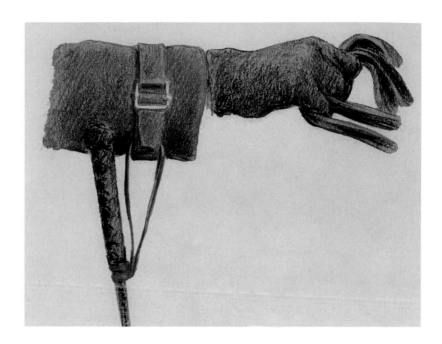

 # Practical Sleeves

I ride a fidgety horse that jumps at the slightest sound and plays with other horses during group rides. He has caused me to drop my whip many times!

I found an old coat that has buckle straps to tighten the sleeves, so I unbuckle one strap, slip it through the wrist strap of my whip and refasten the buckle. Now when I drop my whip, I don't have to dismount to retrieve it because it's still attached to my arm!

....

EFFECTIVE GIRTHING

My horse puffs up his stomach when I saddle him, so by the time I reach the ring, the saddle has rolled and the saddlecloth is flat against his withers. In other words, nothing is where it should be. I have found a trick to prevent this phenomenon from happening. After grooming my horse, I ask a friend to hold up one of his hooves as if to pick it out. Since my horse is too busy trying to keep his balance, he doesn't inflate his stomach. I then gently tighten the girth, and my saddle and saddlecloth stay in place. What a time-saver!

Two Sets of Training Reins

When I'm breaking a young horse, I slip a bridle over a properly adjusted halter and attach a second set of reins to the rings on either side of the halter. I hold the halter reins a bit tighter than the bridle reins to keep control of the horse's head without putting too much pressure on his mouth. My idea is to slowly get him used to the bit without yanking on his mouth. I remove the halter reins once the horse is sufficiently trained to respond to the bit.

A Carrot Instead of a Stick

My mare has the annoying habit of moving at the mounting blocks and won't stand still! Even adjusting the reins when mounting doesn't work. And once I'm in the saddle she still tries to move, which prevents me from adjusting the stirrups or checking the girth. So I use the old carrot trick and it works!

Before I mount my mare, I show her a carrot and give her a piece. I put the rest in my pocket, which she's quite aware of. If she moves once I'm in the saddle, I stop her and immediately give her a piece of carrot. She calmly waits for the third piece of carrot while I make all my necessary adjustments.

My mare completely understood the game after three or four sessions and now she no longer moves. There will soon be no need for the carrot.

A GENTLE MOUTHPIECE

During the breaking stage, some young horses have a hard time accepting a mouthpiece. To get them used to it gently, you can soften the effect of the bit by attaching a second set of reins to their halter. By holding the halter reins tauter than the bridal reins, you can relieve pressure on the mouth while still remaining in control of the animal. Of course, you'll eventually have to remove these extra reins to use a more classic mouthpiece.

A Makeshift Dummy

I own a gentle riding horse that I sometimes use to introduce children to horseback riding. However, some young children find it hard to relax and sit properly in the saddle when they're sitting on a live horse in motion. This is why I sometimes use a makeshift "dummy," which is easy to set up using four straw bales. The bales form a stable pyramid on which I place the saddle. I then attach a set of reins to a tie ring. All the kids need to do is to practice holding onto the reins in a riding position, at the right height and relaxed in the saddle, before trying to ride a live horse.

 # A Bag Full of Tricks

While trail riding, it's not always easy to locate a watering hole accessible to horses. A bucket is too bulky to bring along and difficult to tie to a saddle. So to water my horse I use a clean, large, sturdy plastic bag that I have previously checked for holes. I fill it half full with water and hold it so my horse can drink from it. Get your horse used to drinking from the bag before heading out on a ride. The bag is light, foldable, inexpensive and not bulky!

A RIDE FOR THREE

I use a classic English saddle and I often bring along a second horse when I go for a ride, but it's tiring having to constantly hold his lunge.

My technique consists of keeping the horse on my right-hand side by running the lunge along the front of my saddle and wedging it under my left buttock (so it doesn't bother me by rubbing against my leg). For a better hold, I tie a knot at the end of the lunge, which keeps it from slipping out from under my leg. The lunge must be at least 3 yards (3 m) long so the follower horse has enough slack to lower his head and graze.

I often go on trail rides, but my packhorse is rather stubborn. To prevent the lunge from slipping as soon as he slows down, I wrap the line (once or twice) around the pommel of my western saddle and slide it under my left leg. If my horse pulls too hard or gets excited, I simply stand up to free the lunge. In order to be able to quickly release the lunge and avoid accidents, never tie the lunge securely to yourself or the saddle.

All Lined Up

My friends and I regularly go out on day-long rides, but there's often a lack of trees or space to safely hitch our horses come mealtime. Instead, we tie a highline between two trees. It's very practical, easy to set up and reliable. We can tie several horses to it, giving them freedom to move around.

Make sure to pack about 40 feet (12 m) of rope with a large enough diameter so it's sufficiently heavy and stiff. Tie pieces of twine to the highline to secure the horses (the twine will break if the horses pull too hard). Leave about 6 feet (2 m) between each horse to avoid fights. The highline rope should be knotted tightly around two trees, very taut and at least 6 feet (2 m) from the ground.

MULTIPURPOSE CORD

Every day for the past 9 years, I cover about 9 miles (15 km) on horseback. During my outings I have encountered situations requiring me to hitch my horse, open and close gates while keeping my horse at a distance and deal with broken reins. To handle whatever problems come my way, I have permanently attached a long enough cord fitted with a snap hook to my saddle. The cord is not bulky and is very practical for holding my horse in various positions.

Watering Hole

It's not always easy to find water for my horse to drink when we're out for a ride. However, there's one place in every town and village that's sure to have a water faucet ... the cemetery! As it happens, water is available to visitors who want to fill their watering cans to water flowers on a grave. I leave my horse at the cemetery entrance and discreetly fill a bucket with water for him.

LOST AND FOUND

When I went riding, I wouldn't dare dismount for fear that my horse would run away when I wasn't looking and give me the slip. I found a solution to ease my fears in the "dog accessories" department of my supermarket. As a precaution, I attach a locket to my horse's bridle. The locket houses a piece of paper with my name, address, phone number and horse's name. Now I know he will be returned to me when he is found.

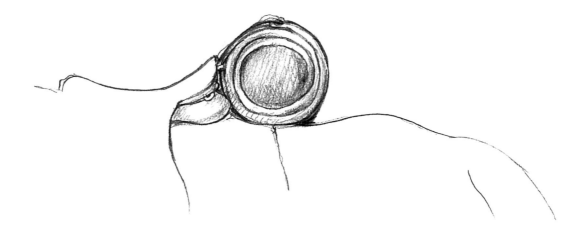

🐴 Saddle Pack

When preparing to go riding, I was never able to load all my supplies (sleeping bag, spare clothes, oilcloth, etc.) onto my horse. So I found a way to save space and compress everything without needing a bag. I use an oilcloth measuring approximately 3 feet x 6 feet (1 m x 2 m). I made three eyelets along the width of the oilcloth through which I passed three laces that serve to hold the rolled up oilcloth. I place my sleeping bag and spare clothes on the oilcloth, roll everything up to form a "sausage" and tie the laces tightly around the bundle. I then use the laces to fasten the bundle to the back of my saddle. My sleeping bag and clothes are protected from the elements and the oilcloth can be converted into a makeshift tent, a ground sheet, a tarp, etc. It's very practical!

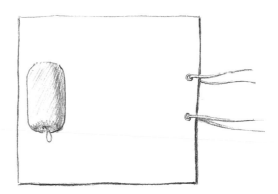

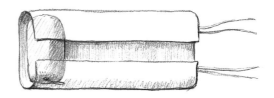

Tail Protection Troubles

My horse must move a lot when he's being trailered because his tail wrap never stays in place and always ends up sliding down his tail. His tail gets damaged and the hairs take forever to grow back.

Most riders fasten a surcingle around their horse's girth and tie the tail wrap strap to the surcingle. In reality, if the horse truly is fidgety (like mine!), the surcingle will slide down the horse's back and the tail wrap will then slide down the tail. It's therefore better to fasten a stirrup leather around the horse's neck and tie the tail wrap strap taut to the stirrup leather. The tail wrap won't budge!

The Proper Attachments

When going on a day-long ride, I always make sure to bring along a good raincoat, just in case. However, I find that the strings that fasten the raincoat to the rings behind the saddle are a nuisance: the knots are hard to untie, the strings occasionally break or sometimes they loosen and my raincoat slips off. In short, they're annoying and my horse isn't a model of patience when I turn in my saddle to deal with the problem! Plus, I end up getting soaked if the strings are being stubborn!

Luckily, I have discovered that synthetic spur straps make ideal attachments. Easy to adjust and remove, they're a very practical solution for attaching my raincoat!

Call Me Anytime

I like bringing my cell phone with me when I go riding in case I need to call for help in an emergency, but my only problem was finding a place to store it. The pockets on riding trousers usually aren't big enough to fit a cell phone and it becomes a burden if I hold it in my hand and a nuisance if I stick it in my belt. However, I easily solved this problem by making an armband that I strap around my upper arm. I slide my cell phone inside the band and I'm ready to go. It's so practical I almost forget it's there!

BULKY HALTER

I love going riding with my friends on summer days. At noon, we stop for a picnic lunch and hitch our horses to trees. The only drawback is that I always have to bring along a halter and lunge to be able to hitch my horse during breaks. The easiest way to save space in my saddlebags is to put the halter on under the bridle, after a few adjustments. The lunge needs to be securely attached so it doesn't come undone. Since a hangman's knot can slide, I choose to use a cavalry knot, which is easy to tie. Form an "S" shaped loop in one hand (not too close to the snap hook or the horse won't be able to extend his neck) and pass the tag end (loose end) of the lunge over the horse's neck and through the top of the "S" loop. Wrap the tag end around the loop, spiraling down four to six times. Pass the tip of the tag end through the bottom loop and tighten. The halter is in place when I remove the bridle and all I have to do is undo the cavalry knot to hitch my horse to a tree.

Protection in the Trailer

September is often the time to bring your horse in from the pasture and get him used to the winter routine of his stall, the ring and his daily work. Of course I take all possible precautions to protect my horse when he's being trailered, but the tail wrap I use has the unfortunate habit of slipping and leaving his tail uncovered. To keep the wrap in place, I wrap it as high as possible around the tail then I lift up a tuft of horsehair, wrap the tail again, lower the tuft and wrap it along with the rest of the tail. This procedure can be repeated further down the tail. The wrap can no longer slip off!

Safety Knot

Riding the trails on a horse that's wearing both a halter and a bridle is very handy since you can hold the horse at the end of a lunge during a well-deserved break. But what should you do with the reins? They could slide off the horse's neck and get stepped on. Once I've dismounted, I pass the reins over my horse's neck, gather them to the right side of his head from below, and slide them up over his head behind his ears, where I use a simple knot to tie the excess reins to the throatlatch. My hands are now free to hold the lunge and enjoy the break!

ELECTRICAL INSULATION

I like to go riding on nice days, but I often come face to face with electric gates without handles. To avoid getting zapped, I bring along a section of inner tube to act as an insulator so I can catch the electrical wire. I can also use the inner tube for other things like temporarily protecting a horse with a girth gall.

Riding Reins

When I'm out for a ride, I often dismount to inspect ditches and embankments. In order for my horse to be able to move his neck around freely while I perform my inspections, I fit the reins with two snap hooks instead of having to unfasten one rein. This is a faster and more practical solution.

TRAINING BRIDGE

TREC is a very cool sport! The only downfall is that riders don't always have the necessary facilities at home to train their horse, especially if they ride a young horse. In order to train at home in my ring, I lined up some pallets and covered them with a wooden board to form a type of bridge. I first tested the setup to make sure it could hold my horse's weight, then I slowly got my horse used to walking on it, first by leading him then by riding him. Now when we're faced with this type of obstacle on a TREC course, everything is so much simpler because my horse has no anxiety about it.

EXCESS REINS

I have long reins that get in my way, and tying the excess with elastics unfortunately doesn't work well. So using a red marker to indicate the start of the excess length (adding 20 inches [50 cm] of wiggle room), I folded the excess, slid it inside an old umbrella cover and wrapped an elastic around the umbrella cover to keep everything in place!

A TREC TRICK

During the Mounted Orienteering phase of a TREC competition, a rider must go from one given point to another at a predetermined speed. The rider needs a map to find the starting point and must be able to judge his horse's speed. Since he's previously timed his horse's speed, he knows the horse can cover 1,640 feet (500 m) in x minutes. He then has to graduate the route on the map in sections of 1,640 feet (500 m) and use his stopwatch to adjust his speed on the course. I turned a strip of clear stiff plastic into a small-scale map-meter in which I punched four holes set half an inch (1 cm) apart, knowing that half an inch (1 cm) equals 820 feet (250 m) on the map. Using two pens, I can then mark the distances on my map, and by pivoting the plastic strip around the pens, I progressively graduate the course. Having marks at every 820 feet (250 m), I can easily adjust my horse's speed on the course.

Find Your Bearings

I love going riding with my mare, but I unfortunately can't always easily find on land something I saw on my map. On more than one occasion I've found myself riding in circles in a forest despite having a very detailed map.

And, while your horse probably has an excellent sense of direction, you can't always rely on it to make to best navigational decisions. Always keep a cell phone on you so you can call for help if necessary.

A SAFETY HANDLE

With the return of warm weather comes the desire to leave the arena behind and hit the trails, to the utmost delight of my horse who shows his exuberance by jumping a little too much for my liking. To avoid falling off, I found another use for my bit converter. When attached to the rings near the saddle pommel, the bit converter becomes a valuable emergency handle if my horse decides to jump or kick. It puts my mind at ease!

🐴 A Drying Rod

Whether we're on the trails or in the ring, my horse loves splashing about in puddles, which often leaves his protective gear wet and dirty. The gear would take forever to dry after being washed and still be damp the next day. It's out of the question to store wet gear directly in a grooming trunk or leave it lying around in the stable hallway, so I came up with the idea of hanging a metal rod from a chain that loops behind the bars on my horse's stall. I hang his shin boots, bell boots, halter, saddlecloth and girth sleeves on the rod, and everything is completely dry the next day. Make sure the rod is well out of reach if your horse tends to grab things!

ESSENTIAL TIPS

PASTURE

DRY FOOD SUPPLIES

To store my horse's food out in the pasture, I went to a D.I.Y. store and bought a watertight plastic food drum meant for soaking fruit, complete with lid and strapping.
If I don't fill it completely to the top, there's room for my horse's pail and a scoop for measuring out his daily ration.

Homemade Flyswatter

My horse can't stand wearing a fly mask. To keep insects away from him while he's in the pasture, I made my own inexpensive flyswatter that won't get tangled in tree branches or stuck on fences. I simply braid strands of baler twine into my horse's forelock. When we go out for a ride, I fasten strands of twine to the browband of his bridle instead and tie knots on the loose ends. It's cheap and effective!

RECYCLING WATER

My horses live in the pasture and since I don't have a water inlet nearby, I regularly have to tow a water container by car to fill the water troughs. What a chore! However, I have found a way to reduce my towing duties. I installed an eaves trough on the roof of the pasture shelter and placed a large garbage can under the spout. I installed a tap in the lower part of the garbage can and can now easily fill a pail with the captured rainwater. I now save on time and water!

Power in a Jug

I use an electric battery that I leave outside to power my pasture fence and have come up with a simple and practical gadget to prevent it from getting damaged by the rain. I cut out the side of a 7 gallon (30 l) plastic jug and placed the energizer inside. This protective shell shelters the energizer from bad weather, and the handle makes it easier to move. I also drilled two holes in the jug to route the ground and line wires through. This contraption prolongs the service life of my electrical equipment and keeps it safe.

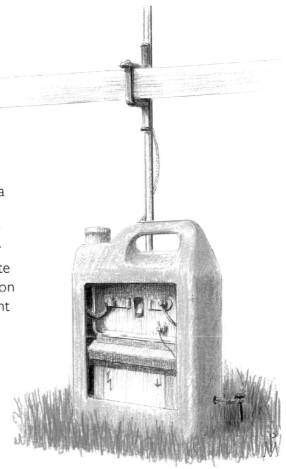

A Quick Way to Roll Up Electric Ribbon

When the nice weather rolls around, pastures often have to be divided into parcels to prevent horses from devouring the spring grass. With rotating parcels of land comes the tedious task of rolling up endless feet of electric ribbon around a spool, but if you hurriedly tangle and kink the ribbon, you risk damaging it and rendering it unfit for use. To keep things simple, use a garden hose reel with a crank. It's much easier to roll up the ribbon, which can then be easily moved and stored.

🐴 Fly Curtain

While out in the pasture, horses are under constant attack by flies and horseflies that irritate and harass them to no end. To provide some relief for my horse, I created a system that works rather well. On a wooden frame I tied a number of strands of cord (or strips of plastic) long enough to reach my horse's breast and upper legs, then I hung the frame from a tree. With a bit of training, my horse has grown used to walking among the strands that swish away the pestering insects, much like the tail of a horse does. It's important to hang this system in your horse's usual rest area. If you have a pasture shelter, you can also hang a cord curtain at the entrance to act as an insect screen.

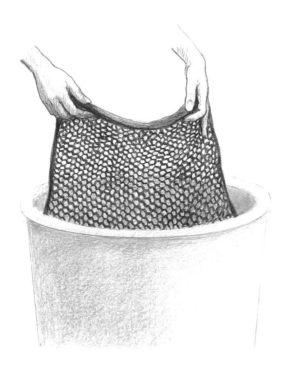

NATURAL FLY REPELLENT

During the summer my horse got covered with flies. This made him nervous and irritable to the point where going for horseback rides was no longer fun. So I found a simple solution at my local drugstore in the form of aniseed. I added a small amount to my horse's daily ration and the result is astonishing (even if it only lasts 1 to 3 days). Don't forget to consult your veterinarian to find out if your horse is allergic to anise.

Insect Repellent Shirt

To ward off insects that pester my mare while she's out in the pasture, a good solution is to rub repellent over her body, but this ends up being costly and loses its effectiveness over time. So I came up with this idea: I dilute insect repellent half and half with water in an air-tight pail. I soak a mesh shirt in the repellent, lightly wring it out and put it on my mare. I store the shirt in a sealed plastic bag to keep it effective for longer and re-soak it in this mixture before each use. It works and is cost effective!

SCREEN SHUTTER

Flies attack my horse even in his stall during summer months, so I came up with this easy solution to give him some reprieve. I made a screen shutter. First, use four wood furring strips to build a frame the size of the shutter, fasten a fine-mesh screen over the frame and place the frame over the stall door. The screen keeps insects out while letting fresh air and sunlight in.

RUST REMOVER

I use an old bathtub as a water trough in my pasture, but the tub tends to rust. My solution for eliminating the rust spots is to rub them with a mixture of lemon juice and salt. The bathtub is almost as good as new.

 # As Clear as Spring Water

When I would go out for a horseback ride, I couldn't understand why my horse would refuse to drink at certain spots. As it turns out, he hates muddy water, so I make sure to point his head upstream, against the current. This way, he won't be drinking muddy water stirred up by his hooves.

Pasture Scratcher

My mare is happy to be back out in the pasture in April, but she's in the habit of rubbing vigorously against tree trunks to the point where she risks injury to herself and damage to the bark. To prevent this, I installed a customized scratcher in the form of a large mat fastened to a tree trunk. Now my mare can safely scratch to her heart's content!

Portable Shower

My horses spend the summer in the pasture and really appreciate a shower on hot days. Since I don't have a water inlet in my pasture, I invented a portable shower. I fill a 1 gallon (5 l) sprayer (available at any D.I.Y. store) with water and use the nozzle to spray my horses. Since the water pressure is controlled by the nozzle, I can spray my horses without spooking them. They're happy to finally get some cooling relief in the field!

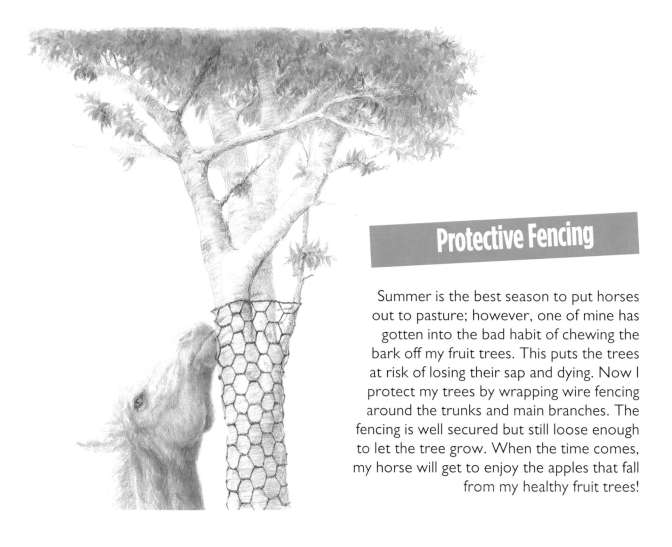

Protective Fencing

Summer is the best season to put horses out to pasture; however, one of mine has gotten into the bad habit of chewing the bark off my fruit trees. This puts the trees at risk of losing their sap and dying. Now I protect my trees by wrapping wire fencing around the trunks and main branches. The fencing is well secured but still loose enough to let the tree grow. When the time comes, my horse will get to enjoy the apples that fall from my healthy fruit trees!

ANTI-DERMATITIS

My horse suffered from summer dermatitis while in pasture. I tried every product sold at specialty stores, but none proved to be an effective remedy. Knowing that insect bites cause this type of dermatitis, I decided to administer an insect repellent to my horse. Every day for a few months prior to the August heat, I mixed 7 ounces (200 g) of raw leeks cut into ½ inch (1 cm) slices into his feed. During the same timeframe, I rubbed the base of his mane and tail with a lemon cut in half. The results were amazing! It's nevertheless important to avoid putting your horse out to pasture on very hot days.

Eliminating Dirt

My horses roll in the mud when they are out in the pasture. Even after hours of grooming, I still can't get it all off. I have three horses and don't have time to spend hours rubbing them clean after my classes, so I found a solution while rummaging through my cosmetics. Moisturizing cream works like a charm; any brand or type (baby cream, hand cream) will do. I apply cream to the muddiest areas and, once the dirt has been removed, I run a wet washcloth over my horse's coat. The hairs are clean and smell nice in 3 seconds flat.

Catching a Pastured Horse

The mare I was supposed to ride wouldn't let me near her so, instead of running after her, I took a pail of water and followed her from a distance while circling the pasture. By doing so, I gradually got close to her and stood slightly in front of her. I let her approach me and put down the pail so she could have a drink. While she was drinking, I buckled the halter around her neck and waited until she lifted her head to slowly slide the rest of halter on her.

TALC TO THE RESCUE

Come winter it's always the same problem. As soon as the temperature becomes humid and the rain makes the ground muddy, my horse develops a serious case of scabies. I've tried a number of treatments, often expensive and ineffective. I decided to put talc on the infection and managed to purchase a large amount at a reasonable price. As soon as the scabs appeared, I cleaned them and applied the talc. It dried out the infection and prevented it from advancing.

CATCH ME IF YOU CAN!

If you have a pastured mare that won't be caught even though you've tried enticing her with a pail of pellets, tempting her with carrots or calmly approaching her without a halter while talking softly to her, try the following tricks.

Walk Backwards

If the mare has a pasture companion, try approaching her with the companion horse attached to a lunge line, but do not look at her because doing so will quickly give away your intentions. If this doesn't work, walk backwards toward her. It works every time. To gain her confidence to the point where you won't have to resort to such trickery, visit her every day without catching her, just to give her a treat. Gradually incorporate a halter into the routine, but still don't attempt to catch her. She'll quickly understand that you're not just approaching her to lead her out of the pasture.

Groundwork

When I work with my 20-year-old mare, I leave her halter and lunge line at the pasture gate (the halter detached from the lunge line) and I casually approach her with treats. I lure her back to the gate, slip on her halter and buckle it at its loosest setting so she's not uncomfortable or frightened. I also work her on the lunge and at liberty, which has boosted her trust in me and has made her much more approachable in the pasture.

The Tissue Trick

Having had this type of problem with my pony, I stumbled upon a solution on a day that I had a cold. After walking into the pasture to groom my pony, I pulled out a pack of tissues from my pocket. Puzzled by the sound, my pony approached me and I easily slid on his halter. Ever since that day, I make sure to carry around an empty pack of tissues.

Fussy Drinkers

Our pastured horses refuse to drink water left for them in a large bathtub because the high iron content in the water alters the taste. Our solution to get them to drink is to add 2 tablespoons of white vinegar to the bathtub filled three-quarters full with water. Very effective!

Death to Thistles!

Every year, my horse's pasture would be invaded by thistles. Instead of endlessly cutting them, I found an environmentally friendly way of killing these plants. Since salt kills plant roots, I cut the thistle stems and pour salt down their hollow shaft.

Storage Solution

I have a pasture shelter where I store my tack, but the walls were too damp to hang anything up on them. To solve this problem, I used old horseshoes and baler twine to hang up my equipment. I hang my halters and bridles on horseshoes nailed to the wall, and I sling my saddle pads and blankets over an old wood batten or a broom stick suspended between two horseshoes fastened to the wall.

A CLEANSING RUBDOWN

Come winter, my pastured horses are often covered in mud. It's nearly impossible to remove mud patches from their legs using a dandy brush, and I'm always afraid that they'll catch mud fever. Don't even think of using a curry comb: its stiff teeth could injure a horse's tendons. While looking through a gardening magazine, I found plastic-lined gloves designed for pruning rose bushes. Now I simply rub my horses' legs with the gloves on and the mud disappears (plus your horse gets a leg massage). Effective and practical!

Oh, the Mud!

Trampled by horses and tractor tires, the ground around my pasture feeder had turned to mud. It wasn't fun sinking knee-deep in muck when I wanted to take Pinpin out for a ride, not to mention the mud-related hoof problems that can occur in such conditions. To start with, my solution was to choose a new location for the feeder near the gate to minimize the formation of tractor tire ruts. I then dug a hole 16 inches (40 cm) deep, laid down some drain tiles to stabilize the soil and improve drainage and filled the hole with gravel. A few inches from the surface, I arranged stones in a flagstone pattern and covered them with gravel and a bit of sand to fill the gaps between the stones. I set the feeder on this base and now my horses can come and eat without sinking in mud!

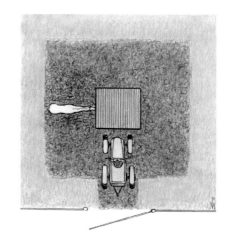

SLUSH

🪨 Stones
▨ Gravel and sand
▮ Soil
○ Drain tile

16 in
(40 cm)

Man Gates

Install man gates in fences to avoid having to constantly open and close the big gates. Man gates are usually 16 inches (40 cm) wide. To prevent colts from getting stuck between the fence posts, install a removable tube or chain (an old dog collar will work just fine) across the man gate to form an H. Remove the tube or chain when you need to walk through the opening, then put it back in its place. Your colts won't be able to fly the coop.

THE LURE OF BREAD!

To entice a horse at the far end of the pasture or one that's hard to catch, shaking a pail of dry bread usually works, but the pail gets in the way when you need to fasten the halter or open and close the gates. To get my horses to come without being hindered by a pail, I carry two slices of very dry bread. Once in the pasture, I rub the slices together to get their attention. The sound of the crusty bread summons them every time. Once they gobble up the treat, my hands are free and I don't have to return to the stables to put the pail away!

QUICK DRY

In April, a horse's hair is still fairly long and the weather can be cold. If your horse has worked up a sweat, it's important to carefully dry him off before returning him to his stall or pasture, but I unfortunately don't always have time to walk my mount to cool him down. To quickly dry my horse, I rub him down with a cloth soaked in camphor alcohol and thoroughly dry his back and loins so he doesn't catch a chill. You can also cover your horse with a blanket if it's cold outside.

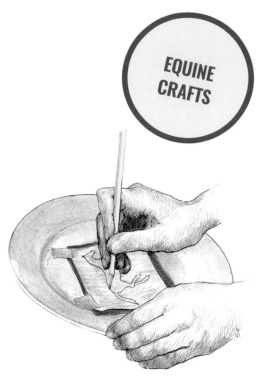

How to Decorate a Plate

What You Need: A porcelain plate, 90 percent rubbing alcohol, tracing paper, carbon paper, felt-tip pens for porcelain, a lead pencil and adhesive tape.

1. Choose a horse drawing with a well-defined outline like one you might find in a comic book. If the drawing is small, photocopy it using an enlarging option to make it bigger. Trace the image on the tracing paper with the pencil.

2. Clean the plate with a cloth soaked in alcohol. Place the black side of the carbon paper onto the plate and tape it in place. Lay the tracing paper on top and retrace the outline of the drawing with the pencil.

3. The drawing is now lightly printed on the plate. Remove the tracing paper and carbon paper and retrace the outline with felt-tip pens. Let the ink dry for 4 hours.

4. Put the plate in a cold oven and set the temperature to 325°F (170°C). Bake for 30 minutes then let the plate cool.

Tip: Hand wash to prevent the drawing from fading.

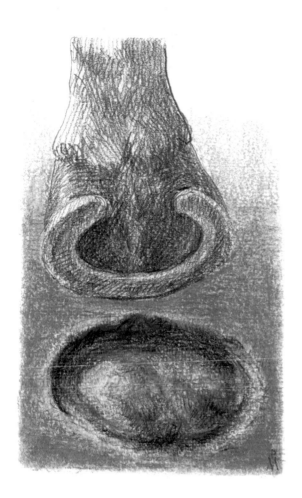

🐴 Hoof Art

To keep my children busy during a school break, I organized a horse-themed casting workshop. The goal was to find a clear hoof print in dry mud, gently clean it with a paintbrush and "immortalize" it in plaster. For this I used casting plaster bought at an arts and crafts store, water, flexible cardboard, string and a container.

First, place a strip of flexible cardboard around the hoof print and tie string around the mold to keep it closed. Stick some matches in the ground along the outside of the mold to prevent the cardboard from moving.

In a container, combine the water and plaster until you get a smooth paste, then pour it over the hoof print. Let it dry for at least an hour before removing the cast and cardboard. The next day, simply separate the cardboard from the plaster cast and paint the hoof print. We now have a cool knickknack that my children made themselves to decorate their room!

INDEX